God's Wisdom
for Women

Topical Scripture
and Encouragement

Patricia Miller *and*
Rachel Gorman

BakerBooks

a division of Baker Publishing Group
Grand Rapids, Michigan

Published by Baker Books
a division of Baker Publishing Group
P.O. Box 6287, Grand Rapids, MI 49516-6287
www.bakerbooks.com

Printed in the United States of America

Library of Congress Cataloging-in-Publication Data

ISBN 978-0-8010-1948-7

17 18 19 20 21 22 23   7 6 5 4 3 2 1

We have this hope as an anchor
for the soul, firm and secure.

Hebrews 6:19 NIV

Topics

 Look for the anchor within each topic. This signifies an "anchor verse" and offers an overview for the topic.

Introduction

I (Rachel) have often struggled with my persona as a woman—at times feeling too feminine, at others too tough. Too weak, but also too strong. Always too much, but never enough. I was insulted for my self-sufficiency or "masculine" strength on the volleyball court, and in the same breath patronized for softness or gentleness. I could never win, never feel free, never sure what I was allowed to do or not do as a woman.

It took me most of my adolescence to truly meet Jesus—bad decisions, misdirection, lies, and chaos followed me through high school and college. It wasn't until the end of college that I could say I truly wanted to *know* Jesus. During this time I read Philip Yancey's excellent book *The Jesus I Never Knew*. I'll never forget reading about what he describes as the "flannel board Jesus."[1]

Somehow I'd missed actually seeing the true character of Jesus for the first twenty-one years of my life. I only saw the flannel board Jesus, packaged neatly for Sunday school—one dimensional and flat. Honestly, looking back, I think I would have admitted that this version of Jesus wasn't someone I really wanted to know or spend time with—and definitely not follow or obey. But then I read these words I'll never forget: "Two words one could never think of applying to the Jesus of the Gospels: boring and predictable. How is it then that the church has tamed such a character—has, in Dorothy Sayers' words, 'very efficiently pared the claws of the

Lion of Judah, certified Him as a fitting household pet for pale curates and pious old ladies'?"[2]

With those words the flannel board was beginning to fade, and I was starting to see the Lion of the Gospels. Jesus as Aslan, the powerful and kind lion in the Chronicles of Narnia books. That was someone I wanted to know.

Too Much and Never Enough

As I began this journey to put away the flannel board Jesus and know the real Jesus, I still struggled to understand which parts of me and my personality were acceptable. As a Christian woman, was I allowed strength *and* femininity? Was I allowed to feel bold *and* gentle? I was trapped by these thoughts—still too much and never enough. The world with its misconceptions, and often other Christians, dictated how I should act and what I should feel. Since all expectations contradicted each other, I was at a loss.

It was when I discovered these powerful words by Dorothy Sayers in her book *Are Women Human?* that I started to finally feel free. Accepted. Wanted. She said,

> Perhaps it is no wonder that the women were first at the Cradle and last at the Cross. They had never known a man like this Man— there never has been such another. A prophet and teacher who never nagged at them, never flattered or coaxed or patronised; who never made arch jokes about them, never treated them either as "The women, God help us!" or "The ladies, God bless them!"; who rebuked without querulousness and praised without condescension; who took their questions and arguments seriously; who never mapped out their sphere for them, never urged them to be feminine or jeered at them for being female; who had no axe to grind and no uneasy male dignity to defend; who took them as he found them and was completely unself-conscious. There is no act, no sermon, no parable in the whole Gospel that borrows its pungency from female perversity; nobody could possibly guess

from the words and deeds of Jesus that there was anything "funny" about woman's nature.[3]

As I read these words, my confusion began to dissipate, and I started to see clearly for the first time. The Jesus Sayers describes, the real Jesus of the Gospels, pulled at all my misconceptions about myself, my world, and Jesus himself. Sayers' words simultaneously showed me two very powerful things: First, I'm not the only woman to feel this dichotomy between who I am and who the world tells me I should be. And second, here is a man I want to know, here is the Jesus who accepts me, frees me, and puts my fears and insecurities to rest. I can trust this man.

Maybe you're like me, always feeling too much and not enough, or maybe you've always understood your place in the world. Maybe you grew up knowing Jesus as a multifaceted, multidimensional hero, or maybe you're longing to put away the Sunday school flannel board and meet the Lion, Jesus.

Whoever you are, no matter how you grew up, what you've experienced, or where you're longing for restoration—I believe we are all looking for *hope*. The longer I live and the more women I begin to truly know, the more I realize that every one of us has experienced sadness, longing, and loneliness. Even if it's hidden and no one else knows—not one of us is exempt. We long for hope.

Anchors and Hope

As we prepared for this book, one visual kept coming to mind: an anchor. Steadfast and mighty, anchors help to tether us through the storm. God's Word is our anchor. Without his promises, we are subject to any storm life gives us. Without an anchor to truth we are in peril—tossed around with no direction, no map, completely at the mercy of the storms that surround us.

We all, each and every one of us, need a strong tether in life; we were created for this very thing—something to help us hold fast to "the hope set before us" (Hebrews 6:18 NIV).

This is the hope promised in God's Word: that God keeps his promises, that we are not alone, and that we can find our hope in the Scriptures through Jesus. "God did this so that, by two unchangeable things in which it is impossible for God to lie, we who have fled to take hold of the hope set before us may be greatly encouraged. We have this hope as an anchor for the soul, firm and secure" (Hebrews 6:18–19 NIV).

How to Use This Book

You can use this book as a topical field guide, a starting place, to help you easily find God's words for your life and your journey. You can discover and read through new topics as you need them, hurry to a specific topic in a moment of crisis, and at other times take the time to pause and reflect for long quiet periods. The book is intended to be an anchor; it's not the whole ocean, or even the ship, but rather a tether to Scripture and a map for journeying deeper into and learning more from the Bible.

Each of these topics literally fills books, sermons, and whole sections of the internet—but God's Word is an essential place to start. Our hope is that this book will lie open on your bedside table, on your desk, on your kitchen counter, next to your Bible— dog-eared, with pen marks and sticky notes marking the pages and verses that your heart and mind need most.

Our hope is that within these pages you see the Jesus of the Bible, the Lion, the Aslan—these are his words. May you find him here, and may it be an anchor for your soul.

Pat and Rachel

 Look for the anchor within each topic. This signifies an "anchor verse," and offers an overview for the topic.

Hebrews 6:18–20 We who have run for our very lives to God have every reason to grab the promised hope with both hands and never let go. It's an unbreakable spiritual lifeline, reaching past all appearances right to the very presence of God where Jesus, running on ahead of us, has taken up his permanent post as high priest for us. (MSG)

Knowing God

We must pay the most careful attention, therefore,

to what we have heard, so that we do not drift away.

Hebrews 2:1 NIV

· The Good News ·

The Gospel That Changes Everything

What makes Christianity unique? How is it different from any other "religion"? The answer is as simple—and as profound—as the difference between *news* and *advice*. The great British pastor, Dr. Martyn Lloyd-Jones, asked his listeners to imagine a village that was about to be attacked by an invading army. At this point, the king could send military advisers to help the villagers ready defenses—dig trenches, collect arms, and prepare for battle. These advisers could help with their good advice.

However, if the king's army had already defeated the enemy invaders *before* they reached the village, he would instead send messengers announcing the report of the victory—the battle was already won.[1] That's *good news*. The *message* of Christianity, the *gospel*, is good *news* (that's what *gospel* means: "good news"). The gospel is not about receiving good advice. It is not about you and what you can do to fix yourself. It is about God and what he has already done in and through Jesus, by the power of the Holy Spirit, to rescue you. The gospel is good news, absolute truth. The battle has already been won! And this good news *changes everything*.

· ·

The gospel is this: We are more sinful and flawed in ourselves than we ever dared believe, yet at the very same time we are more loved and accepted in Jesus Christ than we ever dared hope.[2]

Tim and Kathy Keller

· ·

What the gospel tells us about God:

God is perfectly just and perfectly loving.

> Numbers 14:18 The LORD is slow to anger and filled with unfailing love, forgiving every kind of sin and rebellion. (NLT)

What the gospel tells us about us:

Human beings have rebelled against God's love and come under his just wrath.

> Titus 3:3 For we too were once foolish, disobedient, misled, enslaved to various passions and desires, spending our lives in evil and envy, hateful and hating one another. (NET)

> Ephesians 2:1–3 Once you were dead because of your disobedience and your many sins. You used to live in sin, just like the rest of the world, obeying the devil—the commander of the powers in the unseen world. He is the spirit at work in the hearts of those who refuse to obey God. All of us used to live that way, following the passionate desires and inclinations of our sinful nature. By our very nature we were subject to God's anger, just like everyone else. (NLT)

What the gospel tells us about the rescue:

God, through Jesus, takes the punishment we deserve for our rebellion. In doing so, he keeps his promise to love and still remain just. We receive this rescue by believing the good news and trusting in Jesus, our Rescuer.

> Romans 5:6–8 You see, at just the right time, when we were still powerless, Christ died for the ungodly. Very rarely will anyone die for a righteous person, though for a good person someone might possibly dare to die. But God demonstrates his own love for us in this: While we were still sinners, Christ died for us. (NIV)

Titus 3:4–7 But when the kindness and love of God our Savior appeared, he saved us, not because of righteous things we had done, but because of his mercy. He saved us through the washing of rebirth and renewal by the Holy Spirit, whom he poured out on us generously through Jesus Christ our Savior, so that, having been justified by his grace, we might become heirs having the hope of eternal life. (NIV)

PRACTICAL LIVING

- If you haven't believed, or if you struggle to believe the gospel, then write down the top three things that keep you from believing. Talk to a Christian friend about these things.
- If you do believe the gospel and are trusting Jesus, take a moment to thank God for his amazing love and grace toward you.
- Study Tim Keller's article "The Centrality of the Gospel," available online at GospelInLife.com.
- Ask yourself:
  » Where am I not applying the truth of the gospel in my life and relationships?
  » How would those areas of my life and those relationships look different if I fully applied the gospel in them?
- Read Tim Keller's article "Religion vs. The Gospel," available online at dbcu.org.

RECOMMENDED READING

- *The Prodigal God*. Tim Keller. Penguin.
- *The Gospel*. Greg Gilbert. Crossway.
- *The Story of God's Love for You*. Sally Lloyd-Jones. Zondervan.

· Who Is God? ·

Knowing the God of the Gospel

Who is the God who rescues? The very same God who created everyone and everything. He is the only true God. He alone is the one worthy of our highest love, loyalty, faithfulness, joy, and delight. As human beings, created by God in God's image, we owe God our unwavering love, faithfulness, and obedience. But it is only by relating to God—through love, faithfulness, and obedience— that we are happy and able to feel the joy of who God made us to be. It was for this purpose—relationship—that we were made, and for this purpose that we were rescued.

So what is the God who rescues like? The book of Exodus, in the Bible, tells the story of God's great rescue of his people from slavery in Egypt. Who is this God who rescues his people? This is his answer:

> Then the LORD came down in a cloud and stood there with him; and he called out his own name, Yahweh. The LORD passed in front of Moses, calling out, "Yahweh! The LORD! The God of compassion and mercy! I am slow to anger and filled with un- failing love and faithfulness. I lavish unfailing love to a thousand generations. I forgive iniquity, rebellion, and sin. But I do not excuse the guilty."
>
> Exodus 34:5–7 NLT

In this one passage, we get a microburst of revelation about who God is and what he is like, but it takes the entire Bible to reveal even more fully the God of the gospel, the God who rescues.

· ·

If you want joy, power, peace, eternal life, you must get close to, or even into, the thing that has them. They are not a sort of prize which God could, if He chose, just hand out to anyone. . . . Once a man is separated from God, what can he do but wither and die?[1]

C. S. Lewis

· ·

God is Spirit.

John 4:23–24 But a time is coming—and now is here—when the true worshipers will worship the Father in spirit and truth, for the Father seeks such people to be his worshipers. God is spirit, and the people who worship him must worship in spirit and truth. (NET)

God is the only true God; there is no one like him.

Jeremiah 10:6 There is none like you, O LORD; you are great, and your name is great in might. (ESV)

Deuteronomy 6:4–5 "Attention, Israel! GOD, our God! GOD the one and only! Love GOD, your God, with your whole heart: love him with all that's in you, love him with all you've got!" (MSG)

God is personal. He speaks; he has a name.

Exodus 3:14 God said to Moses, "I AM WHO I AM. This is what you are to say to the Israelites: 'I AM has sent me to you.'" (NIV)

· ·

Do you feel loved by God because you believe he makes much of you, or because you believe he frees you and empowers you to enjoy making much of him? It is the difference between the modern world where all terminates on self, and the biblical world where all terminates on God.[2]

John Piper

. . . .

God is triune.

The Father is God:

> Genesis 17:1 When Abram was ninety-nine years old the LORD appeared to Abram and said to him, "I am God Almighty; walk before me, and be blameless." (ESV)

The Son, Jesus, is God:

> Colossians 2:9 For in Christ lives all the fullness of God in a human body. (NLT)

The Holy Spirit is God:

> 2 Corinthians 13:14 The grace of the Lord Jesus Christ and the love of God and the fellowship of the Holy Spirit be with you all. (ESV)

God is eternal, all-knowing, all-powerful, and everywhere present.

> Psalm 90:2 Even before the mountains came into existence, or you brought the world into being, you were the eternal God. (NET)

> Psalm 147:4–5 He determines the number of the stars and calls them each by name. Great is our Lord and mighty in power; his understanding has no limit. (NIV)

> Jeremiah 32:17–18 O Sovereign LORD! You made the heavens and earth by your strong hand and powerful arm. Nothing is too hard for you! . . . You are the great and powerful God, the LORD of Heaven's Armies. (NLT)

Psalm 139:7–12 I can never escape from your Spirit! I can never get away from your presence! If I go up to heaven, you are there; if I go down to the grave, you are there. If I ride the wings of the morning, if I dwell by the farthest oceans, even there your hand will guide me, and your strength will support me. I could ask the darkness to hide me and the light around me to become night—but even in darkness I cannot hide from you. To you the night shines as bright as day. Darkness and light are the same to you. (NLT)

What is God? . . . God is the creator and sustainer of everyone and everything. He is eternal, infinite, and unchangeable in his power and perfection, goodness and glory, wisdom, justice, and truth. Nothing happens except through him and by his will.[3]

Tim Keller and Sam Shammas

God is holy, just, integral, whole—lacking in nothing.

Isaiah 6:3 They were calling out to each other, "Holy, holy, holy is the LORD of Heaven's Armies! The whole earth is filled with his glory!" (NLT)

Deuteronomy 32:4 The Rock, his work is perfect [whole, complete], for all his ways are justice. A God of faithfulness and without iniquity, just and upright is he. (ESV)

Acts 17:24–25 The God who made the world and everything in it, being Lord of heaven and earth, does not live in temples made by man, nor is he served by human hands, as though he needed anything, since he himself gives to all mankind life and breath and everything. (ESV)

God is love.

1 John 4:7–10 Dear friends, let us love one another, for love comes from God. Everyone who loves has been born of God and knows God. Whoever does not love does not know God, because God is love. This is how God showed his love among us: He sent his one and only Son into the world that we might live through him. This is love: not that we loved God, but that he loved us and sent his Son as an atoning sacrifice for our sins. (NIV)

God is full of grace and mercy.

 Ephesians 2:4–5 But because of his great love for us, God, who is rich in mercy, made us alive with Christ even when we were dead in transgressions—it is by grace you have been saved. (NIV)

God is the Creator and Sustainer of his good creation.

Genesis 1:1 First this: God created the Heavens and Earth—all you see, all you don't see. (MSG)

Genesis 1:31 Then God looked over all he had made, and he saw that it was very good! (NLT)

Hebrews 1:3 The Son is the radiance of God's glory and the exact representation of his being, sustaining all things by his powerful word. (NIV)

PRACTICAL LIVING

• Select one or two verses from this topic that particularly spoke to you. Look them up and read in context. Read each verse several times, carefully thinking through each word. Ask yourself: *What does this teach me about God? How does this truth help me treasure God?*

- Join a church, small group, or Bible study where people are enthralled by God's goodness, beauty, and truth.
- Find and listen to music, songs, or hymns that speak of God's character.
- Study the list of God's characteristics in Appendix A.

RECOMMENDED READING

- *None Like Him: 10 Ways God Is Different from Us.* Jen Wilken. Crossway.
- *Knowing God.* J. I. Packer. IVP.
- *The Mind of the Maker.* Dorothy Sayers. HarperCollins.
- *God: As He Longs for You to See Him.* Chip Ingram. Baker.

· How to Know God ·
Living in the Gospel

How does the gospel transform us? How does it change us and help us to grow? The way to grow in the gospel is *through* the gospel. We grow in the gospel as we work the truth of the gospel deeper and deeper into the core of who we are, in such a way that it begins to transform every aspect of our lives.

This process of working the gospel deeper and deeper into our lives is empowered by the same grace that rescues us. The grace that saves is the same grace that transforms. Growing in the gospel, then, is not a matter of getting beyond grace or adding something to grace but of establishing patterns and habits that are regularly put in place to receive the grace that God gives. These patterns are often referred to as "spiritual disciplines," "means of grace," or "habits of grace."

In his book, *Habits of Grace*, David Mathis points out that while there are many different practices that can help us grow in grace, there are three in particular that are vital: Bible reading, prayer, and being a part of a local church.[1]

. . . .

"The essence of the Christian life," writes John Piper, "is learning to fight for joy in a way that does not replace grace." We cannot earn God's grace or make it flow apart from his free gift. But we can position ourselves to go on getting as he keeps on giving. We can "fight to walk in the paths where he has promised his blessings." We can ready ourselves to remain receivers along his regular routes, sometimes called "the spiritual disciplines," or even better, "the means of grace."[2]

David Mathis

. . . .

Read and study the Bible.

2 Timothy 3:16–17 All Scripture is breathed out by God and profitable for teaching, for reproof, for correction, and for training in righteousness, that the man of God may be complete, equipped for every good work. (ESV)

 Joshua 1:8 Study this Book of Instruction continually. Meditate on it day and night so you will be sure to obey everything written in it. Only then will you prosper and succeed in all you do. (NLT)

26

Psalm 1:2–3 You thrill to GOD's Word, you chew on Scripture day and night. You're a tree replanted in Eden, bearing fresh fruit every month, Never dropping a leaf, always in blossom. (MSG)

Romans 15:4 For whatever was written in former days was written for our instruction, that through endurance and through the encouragement of the Scriptures we might have hope. (ESV)

Establish rhythms of prayer.

Colossians 4:2 Be devoted to prayer, keeping alert in it with thanksgiving. (NET)

Acts 2:42 And they devoted themselves . . . to the breaking of bread and the prayers. (ESV)

1 Thessalonians 5:16–18 Rejoice always, pray continually, give thanks in all circumstances; for this is God's will for you in Christ Jesus. (NIV)

Philippians 4:6 Do not be anxious about anything. Instead, in every situation, through prayer and petition with thanksgiving, tell your requests to God. (NET)

Be a part of a local church.

Hebrews 10:25 And let us not neglect our meeting together, as some people do, but encourage one another, especially now that the day of his return is drawing near. (NLT)

Acts 2:42 And they devoted themselves to the apostles' teaching and the fellowship, to the breaking of bread and the prayers. (ESV)

PRACTICAL LIVING

- Set aside regular time to read the Bible. There are lots of different reading plans available online. Bible.com is a great place to start. See Appendix B.
- Use Psalms 4 and 5 to start a pattern of evening and morning prayer. Read and pray Psalm 4 each evening and Psalm 5 each morning. Also consider working through the Psalms as a guide to prayer, using a book like *The Songs of Jesus* by Tim and Kathy Keller.
- Use a daily devotional book such as Paul David Tripp's *New Morning Mercies*.
- Find a healthy, gospel-centered local church and make full involvement in the church community a central priority with your time, finances, service, and affection.

RECOMMENDED READING

- *Habits of Grace*. David Mathis. Crossway.
- *The Spirit of the Disciplines*. Dallas Willard. HarperOne.
- *Spiritual Disciplines for the Christian Life*. Donald Whitney. NavPress.
- *Prayer: Experiencing Awe and Intimacy with God*. Tim Keller. Penguin.
- *The Songs of Jesus: A Year of Daily Devotions in the Psalms*. Tim and Kathy Keller. Viking.

· Why the Bible? ·
The Story of the Gospel

The Bible is one big book made up of sixty-six smaller books written in different places and times over hundreds of years. It includes prophecies and poems, letters and laws, but it all tells one grand story: the story of the gospel, the good news of God's rescue and restoration. The story unfolds in the Bible in four big sections: creation, fall, redemption, and new creation. In creation (Genesis 1–2) we see what *ought to be*. In the fall (Genesis 3), we see what *is*. Sin has entered God's good world, and all is not as it *ought* to be any longer. In redemption (Genesis 4–Revelation 20) we see what *can be* in light of the rescue that God has launched to save his people from sin. In the new creation (Revelation 21–22), we get a glimpse of what *will be* one day when God restores all things.

. . . .

Now, some people think the Bible is a book of rules, telling you what you should and shouldn't do. The Bible certainly does have some rules in it. They show you how life works best. But the Bible isn't mainly about you and what you should be doing. It's about God and what he has done. . . . the Bible isn't a book of rules, or a book of heroes. The Bible is most of all a Story. It's an adventure story about a young Hero who comes from a far country to win back his lost treasure. It's a love story about a brave Prince who leaves his palace, his throne—everything—to rescue the ones he loves. It's like the most wonderful of fairy tales that has come true in real life! You see, the best thing about this Story is—it's true.[1]

Sally Lloyd-Jones

. . . .

29

Creation

Genesis 1:1 In the beginning God created the heavens and the earth. (NIV)

Genesis 1:31 God saw all that he had made, and it was very good. And there was evening, and there was morning—the sixth day. (NIV)

Fall

Genesis 2:15–17 The Lord God took the man and put him in the Garden of Eden to work it and take care of it. And the Lord God commanded the man, "You are free to eat from any tree in the garden; but you must not eat from the tree of the knowledge of good and evil, for when you eat from it you will certainly die." (NIV)

Genesis 3:8–13 Then the man and his wife heard the sound of the Lord God as he was walking in the garden in the cool of the day, and they hid from the Lord God among the trees of the garden. But the Lord God called to the man, "Where are you?" He answered, "I heard you in the garden, and I was afraid because I was naked; so I hid." And he said, "Who told you that you were naked? Have you eaten from the tree that I commanded you not to eat from?" The man said, "The woman you put here with me—she gave me some fruit from the tree, and I ate it." Then the Lord God said to the woman, "What is this you have done?" The woman said, "The serpent deceived me, and I ate." (NIV)

Redemption

John 3:16 For this is the way God loved the world: He gave his one and only Son, so that everyone who believes in him will not perish but have eternal life. (NET)

 Titus 3:3–7 At one time we too were foolish, disobedient, deceived and enslaved by all kinds of passions and pleasures. We lived in

malice and envy, being hated and hating one another. But when the kindness and love of God our Savior appeared, he saved us, not because of righteous things we had done, but because of his mercy. He saved us through the washing of rebirth and renewal by the Holy Spirit, whom he poured out on us generously through Jesus Christ our Savior, so that, having been justified by his grace, we might become heirs having the hope of eternal life. (NIV)

New Creation

Revelation 21:1–5 Then I saw a new heaven and a new earth, for the first heaven and earth had ceased to exist, and the sea existed no more. And I saw the holy city—the new Jerusalem—descending out of heaven from God, made ready like a bride adorned for her husband. And I heard a loud voice from the throne saying: "Look! The residence of God is among human beings. He will live among them, and they will be his people, and God himself will be with them. He will wipe away every tear from their eyes, and death will not exist any more—or mourning, or crying, or pain, for the former things have ceased to exist." And the one seated on the throne said: "Look! I am making all things new!" (NET)

PRACTICAL LIVING

- Read Genesis 1–3; Romans 5–8; and Revelation 21–22. Summarize the themes you see in these chapters.
- Use the creation (ought), fall (is), redemption (can), and new creation (will) lens to think through everyday topics and situations. For example, in your work, ask: *What ought to be here? What is? What's not working right? What can be? What will be?*
- Spend some time reading and enjoying *The Jesus Storybook Bible* by Sally-Lloyd Jones. This book is beautifully illustrated

and does a wonderful job telling the creation, fall, redemption, and new creation story.

RECOMMENDED READING

- *The Story of God's Love For You.* Sally Lloyd-Jones. Zondervan.
- *The God Who Is There.* D. A. Carson. Baker.
- *Women of the Word: How To Study the Bible with Both Our Hearts and Our Minds.* Jen Wilkin. Crossway.

· What to Do with Doubt ·
How the Gospel Answers Doubt

It's possible to have faith, but to still doubt—these two things are not mutually exclusive. Doubt is not unbelief. Doubt is asking questions about uncertainties from the standpoint of faith. In his book *Doubting,* Alister McGrath makes some helpful distinctions about what doubt is and what it isn't. He explains, "Doubt isn't skepticism—the decision to doubt everything deliberately, as a matter of principle." Nor, he says, is doubt "unbelief—the decision not to have faith in God. Unbelief is an act of the will, rather than a difficulty in understanding."[1]

Whether you consider yourself a believer, a skeptic, or something in between, everyone has faith. We all rest our lives on assumptions that are very difficult to prove to someone who doesn't already share those assumptions with us. Doubts—rather than being an

enemy of faith—can help us grow in our confidence in the hope
that is offered to us in Jesus.

. . . .

If you don't have doubts you're either kidding yourself or
asleep. Doubts are ants in the pants of faith: they keep it awake
and moving.[2]

Frederick Buechner

. . . .

We can find comfort in the midst of doubt.

Mark 9:24 I do believe; help me overcome my unbelief! (NIV)

Jude 22 Be merciful to those who doubt. (NIV)

1 John 4:4–5 You are from God, little children, and have conquered them, because the one who is in you is greater than the one
who is in the world. They are from the world; therefore they speak
from the world's perspective and the world listens to them. (NET)

Even in doubt, there is reason to hope.

John 6:66–69 From this time many of his disciples turned back
and no longer followed him. "You do not want to leave too, do
you?" Jesus asked the Twelve. Simon Peter answered him, "Lord, to
whom shall we go? You have the words of eternal life. We have come
to believe and to know that you are the Holy One of God." (NIV)

John 20:27 Then he [Jesus] said to Thomas, "Put your finger
here; see my hands. Reach out your hand and put it into my side.
Stop doubting and believe." (NIV)

33

It's important to beware of unbelief.

Hebrews 3:19–4:1 So we see that they were not able to enter, because of their unbelief. Therefore, since the promise of entering his rest still stands, let us be careful that none of you be found to have fallen short of it. (NIV)

 2 Corinthians 10:5 We demolish arguments and every pretension that sets itself up against the knowledge of God, and we take captive every thought to make it obedient to Christ. (NIV)

PRACTICAL LIVING

- Write out the doubts you are experiencing. Talk with a Christian friend or pastor about the specific doubts you have. You are probably not alone in your doubts. Knowing others have wrestled with the same kinds of questions can be deeply helpful.

- When you start experiencing doubt, ask yourself: *Do I want to believe and is there something that is holding me back? Or Do I not want to believe and am I looking for reasons to disbelieve?*

- Remember: seasons of doubt and questioning are normal in the journey to trust Jesus and in a life following him. Don't despair when you experience doubt; see it as an opportunity to grow.

RECOMMENDED READING

- *Doubting.* Alister McGrath. IVP.
- *The Reason for God.* Tim Keller. Penguin.
- *Mere Christianity.* C. S. Lewis. HarperOne.
- *When Life and Beliefs Collide.* Carolyn Custis James. Zondervan.

· Sin and God's · Forgiveness

Understanding the Gospel

The gospel is the good news—God in Jesus, by the power of the Holy Spirit, rescues his people from their sin and its consequences. To understand what we've been rescued from and what we continue to fight, we have to understand something about sin, temptation, and forgiveness. We often think about sin as breaking a rule or commandment—but sin is always the rejection of a person before it is the breaking of a rule. Temptation is feeling sin's allure. To be clear: experiencing temptation is not sin. Jesus was tempted but did not sin (Hebrews 4:15). But temptation, if not resisted, will lead us to sin. Until Jesus returns and makes all things new (Revelation 21:1–5), we will not be completely free from sin. But the good news is this—even when we do sin, there is forgiveness, because of Jesus's sacrifice on the cross.

Sin is a rejection of God and separates us from him.

Isaiah 1:4 Oh, what a sinful nation they are—loaded down with a burden of guilt. They are evil people, corrupt children who have rejected the LORD. They have despised the Holy One of Israel and turned their backs on him. (NLT)

Romans 3:10–12 As it is written: There is no one righteous, not even one; there is no one who understands; there is no one who seeks God. All have turned away, they have together become worthless; there is no one who does good, not even one. (NIV)

Isaiah 59:2 But your iniquities have separated you from your God; your sins have hidden his face from you, so that he will not hear. (NIV)

Temptation is an experience of sin's deadly allure and must be resisted at all cost.

James 1:13–15 Let no one say when he is tempted, "I am being tempted by God," for God cannot be tempted with evil, and he himself tempts no one. But each person is tempted when he is lured and enticed by his own desire. Then desire when it has conceived gives birth to sin, and sin when it is fully grown brings forth death. (ESV)

Hebrews 12:4 In your struggle against sin, you have not yet resisted to the point of shedding your blood. (NIV)

James 4:7 Submit yourselves, then, to God. Resist the devil, and he will flee from you. (NIV)

Forgiveness is always offered to us when we look to God in faith.

1 John 2:1–2 My dear children, I write this to you so that you will not sin. But if anybody does sin, we have an advocate with the Father—Jesus Christ, the Righteous One. He is the atoning sacrifice for our sins, and not only for ours but also for the sins of the whole world. (NIV)

 Romans 8:1–3 Therefore, there is now no condemnation for those who are in Christ Jesus, because through Christ Jesus the law of the Spirit who gives life has set you free from the law of sin and death. For what the law was powerless to do because it was weakened by the flesh, God did by sending his own Son in the likeness of sinful flesh to be a sin offering. (NIV)

Acts 13:38 Therefore, my friends, I want you to know that through
Jesus the forgiveness of sins is proclaimed to you. (NIV)

What is sin? Sin is:
The glory of God not honored.
The holiness of God not reverenced.
The greatness of God not admired.
The power of God not praised.
The truth of God not sought.
The wisdom of God not esteemed.
The beauty of God not treasured.
The goodness of God not savored.
The faithfulness of God not trusted.
The promises of God not believed.
The commandments of God not obeyed.
The justice of God not respected.
The wrath of God not feared.
The grace of God not cherished.
The presence of God not prized.
The person of God not loved.[1]

John Piper

PRACTICAL LIVING

- Study Appendix E, "What Does God Do with Forgiven Sin?"
- Memorize Romans 5:8.
- See related topics: Guilt and Forgiving Others.

RECOMMENDED READING

. . . .

- *The Prodigal God.* Tim Keller. Penguin.
- *Not the Way It's Supposed to Be.* Cornelius Plantinga Jr. Eerdmans.
- *Overcoming Sin and Temptation.* John Owen and Kelly Kapic. Crossway.

Encouragement

Comfort

Contentment

Hope

Rest

Self-Worth

Trials

Trust

Cling to your faith in Christ, and keep your conscience clear. For some people have deliberately violated their consciences; as a result, their faith has been shipwrecked.

1 Timothy 1:19 NLT

· Comfort ·

There's comfort to be found when we submit to the plan of One who's wiser, and peace in following wisdom profoundly better than our own.[1]

Paul Tripp

God's Word provides comfort.

 Psalm 119:49–50 Remember your promise to me; it is my only hope. Your promise revives me; it comforts me in all my troubles. (NLT)

God's promise of protection provides comfort.

Psalm 23:4 Even when I walk through the darkest valley, I will not be afraid, for you are close beside me. Your rod and your staff protect and comfort me. (NLT)

Isaiah 51:12–13 I, yes I, am the one who comforts you. So why are you afraid of mere humans, who wither like the grass and disappear? Yet you have forgotten the LORD, your Creator, the one who stretched out the sky like a canopy and laid the foundations of the earth. (NLT)

Jesus himself offers comfort.

2 Thessalonians 2:16–17 Now may our Lord Jesus Christ Himself and God our Father, who has loved us and given us eternal

comfort and good hope by grace, comfort and strengthen your hearts in every good work and word. (NASB)

Our great comforter is the Holy Spirit.

John 14:26–27 The Holy Spirit—he will teach you everything and will remind you of everything I have told you. I am leaving you with a gift—peace of mind and heart. And the peace I give is a gift the world cannot give. So don't be troubled or afraid. (NLT)

Romans 8:26–28 The Holy Spirit helps us in our weakness. . . . We don't know what God wants us to pray for. But the Holy Spirit prays for us with groanings that cannot be expressed in words. And the Father who knows all hearts knows what the Spirit is saying, for the Spirit pleads for us believers in harmony with God's own will. And we know that God causes everything to work together for the good of those who love God and are called according to his purpose for them. (NLT)

God comforts us; we must comfort others.

2 Corinthians 1:3–4 Praise be to the God and Father of our Lord Jesus Christ, the Father of compassion and the God of all comfort, who comforts us in all our troubles, so that we can comfort those in any trouble with the comfort we ourselves receive from God. (NIV)

PRACTICAL LIVING

- Each day on a calendar page, write a way that God has brought you comfort.
- Look for practical ways to bring comfort to others, as expressed in 2 Corinthians 1:2–5.
- Memorize Isaiah 26:3.

- Study the "Names of God" list and what his names mean in Appendix C.

RECOMMENDED READING

- *Walking with God through Pain and Suffering.* Tim Keller. Penguin.
- *Comforts from the Cross.* Elyse Fitzpatrick. Crossway.
- *Daily Reflections on the Names of God.* Ava Pennington. Revell.
- *The Jesus I Never Knew.* Philip Yancey. Zondervan.
- *Suffering and the Heart of God.* Diane Langberg. New Growth.

· Contentment ·

Contentment is not finally getting to a place of peace and rest when all is complete, accomplished, finalized, or safe. Contentment comes in the midst of the mess and pressures of life—the quiet confidence and assurance that God is in control.

Contentment is relying on God no matter the circumstances.

Isaiah 26:3 You will keep in perfect peace those whose minds are steadfast, because they trust in you. (NIV)

2 Corinthians 12:9–10 And He has said to me, "My grace is sufficient for you, for power is perfected in weakness." Most gladly,

therefore, I will rather boast about my weaknesses, so that the power of Christ may dwell in me. Therefore I am well content with weaknesses, with insults, with distresses, with persecutions, with difficulties, for Christ's sake; for when I am weak, then I am strong. (NASB)

Contentment comes from knowing and accepting that God is in control.

Isaiah 25:1 O LORD, You are my God; I will exalt You, I will give thanks to Your name; For You have worked wonders, Plans formed long ago, with perfect faithfulness. (NASB)

Isaiah 42:16 I will lead the blind by a way they do not know, in paths they do not know I will guide them. I will make darkness into light before them and rugged places into plains. These are the things I will do, and I will not leave them undone. (NASB)

Know that God created us and plans for our future.

Jeremiah 29:11 For I know the plans I have for you, declares the LORD, plans for welfare and not for evil, to give you a future and a hope. (ESV)

Isaiah 43:1 But now, this is what the LORD says . . . "Do not fear, for I have redeemed you; I have summoned you by name; you are mine." (NIV)

I want to cultivate a deep sense of gratitude, of groundedness, or enough, even while I'm longing for something more. The longing and the gratitude, both. I'm practicing believing that God knows more than I know, that he sees what I can't, that he's weaving a future I can't even imagine.[1]

Shauna Niequist

44

Contentment is a choice.

> Psalm 131:2 But I have calmed and quieted my soul, like a weaned child with its mother; like a weaned child is my soul within me. (ESV)

> Philippians 4:11–13 For I have learned to be satisfied with what I have. I know what it is to be in need and what it is to have more than enough. I have learned this secret, so that anywhere, at any time, I am content, whether I am full or hungry, whether I have too much or too little. I have the strength to face all conditions by the power that Christ gives me. (GNT)

We are called to be content with our material possessions.

> Hebrews 13:5 Keep your lives free from the love of money, and be satisfied with what you have. For God has said, "I will never leave you; I will never abandon you." (GNT)

> 1 Timothy 6:6–8 Yet true godliness with contentment is itself great wealth. After all, we brought nothing with us when we came into the world, and we can't take anything with us when we leave it. So if we have enough food and clothing, let us be content. (NLT)

Be content, even when others have more.

> Psalm 37:7, 16 Be patient and wait for the LORD to act; don't be worried about those who prosper or those who succeed in their evil plans. . . . The little that a good person owns is worth more than the wealth of all the wicked. (GNT)

. . . .

It's obvious then that covetousness is exactly the opposite of faith. It's the loss of contentment in Christ so that we start to crave other things to satisfy the longings of our hearts.[2]

John Piper

. . . .

PRACTICAL LIVING

- Take a break from social media sites, such as Instagram, Pinterest, and Facebook. How does this change your outlook and view on contentment?
- Volunteer at a mission, homeless shelter, orphanage, hospital, or nursing home. Work at bringing joy to others.
- Purchase a small notebook, and keep a list of specific things God does for you and has given you.
- Memorize Psalm 29:11.
- Give away things that you no longer wear or need. Do you collect things for security?
- Study the biblical term "blessed." Every time you read "blessed" think "content." In Scripture, "blessedness" equals "contentment."

RECOMMENDED READING

- *Choosing Gratitude*. Nancy Leigh DeMoss. Moody.
- *Discontentment*. Lou Priolo. P&R.
- *One Thousand Gifts: A Dare to Live Fully Right Where You Are*. Ann Voskamp. Zondervan.
- *The Rare Jewel of Christian Contentment*. Jeremiah Burroughs. Sovereign Grace.
- *An Experimental Mutiny Against Excess*. Jen Hatmaker. B&H.

· Hope ·

A biblical view of eternity brings the Christian genuine hope in any situation, and hope produces insight and courage. Everything God calls us to do with our hearts and our hands looks to the sure reality of eternity.[1]

Paul Tripp

God is our only true source of hope.

Psalm 71:5–6 For you, O LORD, are my hope, my trust, O LORD, from my youth. Upon you I have leaned from before my birth; you are he who took me from my mother's womb. My praise is continually of you. (ESV)

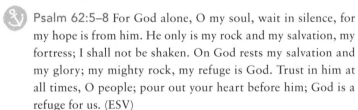 Psalm 62:5–8 For God alone, O my soul, wait in silence, for my hope is from him. He only is my rock and my salvation, my fortress; I shall not be shaken. On God rests my salvation and my glory; my mighty rock, my refuge is God. Trust in him at all times, O people; pour out your heart before him; God is a refuge for us. (ESV)

Psalm 43:5 Why are you cast down, O my soul, and why are you in turmoil within me? Hope in God; for I shall again praise him, my salvation and my God. (ESV)

Hope rests in the truth of God's Word.

Psalm 130:5 I am counting on the LORD; yes, I am counting on him. I have put my hope in his word. (NLT)

Express hope, or lack of hope, through prayer.

Romans 8:24–27 (If we already have something, we don't need to hope for it. But if we look forward to something we don't yet have, we must wait patiently and confidently.) And the Holy Spirit helps us in our weakness. For example, we don't know what God wants us to pray for. But the Holy Spirit prays for us with groanings that cannot be expressed in words. And the Father who knows all hearts knows what the Spirit is saying, for the Spirit pleads for us believers in harmony with God's own will. (NLT)

Romans 12:12 Rejoice in our confident hope. Be patient in trouble, and keep on praying. (NLT)

. . . .

We need a living hope to get through life and endure suffering. A living hope enables us to have both sorrow and joy. Our living hope is an inheritance achieved for us by Christ.[2]

Tim Keller

. . . .

Cling to this hope: God has a plan!

Jeremiah 29:11 "For I know the plans I have for you," declares the LORD, "plans to prosper you and not to harm you, plans to give you hope and a future." (NIV)

Lamentations 3:21–23 This I recall to my mind, therefore I have hope. The LORD's lovingkindnesses indeed never cease, for His compassions never fail. They are new every morning; great is Your faithfulness. (NASB)

PRACTICAL LIVING
. . . .

- Study A. W. Tozer's book, *The Attributes of God.* Make a list of those characteristics. See Appendix A for a place to start.

Benefits of Hope

Confidence (Philippians 1:20)
Joy through testing (Romans 12:12; 1 Thessalonians 4:13)
Greater faith and love (Colossians 1:4–5)
Perseverance (Romans 8:24–25)
Steadfastness (1 Thessalonians 1:3)
Increased energy and passion (1 Timothy 4:10)
Purity of life (1 John 3:3)
Closer relationship with the Father (Hebrews 7:19)
Security (Hebrews 6:19)

- Study the list of God's names in Appendix C. Each has a meaning that helps us know the God of hope.
- As you speak with others, practice instilling hope with your words (positive, encouraging, affirming, and gospel-filled).
- Memorize Psalm 62:5–8. Use it as your home screen on your phone, or post it around your home.
- Get a ring or bracelet that can be a special reminder that there is hope in every situation because of Christ's work on the cross.

RECOMMENDED READING

- *Gaining a Hopeful Spirit*. Joni Eareckson Tada. Rose.
- *From Despair to Hope*. Peter Williams. Day One.
- *God: As He Longs for You to See Him*. Chip Ingram. Baker.
- *The Broken Way*. Ann Voskamp. Zondervan.

· Rest ·

Rest is a decision we make. Rest is choosing to do nothing when we have too much to do, slowing down when we feel pressure to go faster, stopping instead of starting. Rest is listening to our weariness and responding to our tiredness, not to what is making us tired. Rest is the result of the humiliating recognition that we are not necessary. Rest is what happens when we say one simple word: "No!" Rest is the ultimate humiliation, because in order to rest we must admit we are not necessary, that the world can get along without us, that God's work does not depend on us.[1]

Mike Yaconelli

Rest is a person, not an activity.

Matthew 11:27–30 Jesus resumed talking to the people, but now tenderly. . . . "Are you tired? Worn out? Burned out on religion? Come to me. Get away with me and you'll recover your life. I'll show you how to take a real rest. Walk with me and work with me—watch how I do it. Learn the unforced rhythms of grace. I won't lay anything heavy or ill-fitting on you. Keep company with me and you'll learn to live freely and lightly." (MSG)

Matthew 12:6–8 [Jesus said:] "I tell you that something greater than the temple is here. If you had known what these words mean, 'I desire mercy, not sacrifice,' you would not have condemned the innocent. For the Son of Man is Lord of the Sabbath." (NIV)

You don't just need rest. You need the Lord of Rest.[2]

Bill Gorman

The God who never tires gave us an example of rest, a pattern to follow.

> Genesis 2:2–3 By the seventh day God had finished the work he had been doing; so on the seventh day he rested from all his work. Then God blessed the seventh day and made it holy, because on it he rested from all the work of creating that he had done. (NIV)

Rest is commanded.

> Exodus 20:8–11 Observe the Sabbath day, to keep it holy. Work six days and do everything you need to do. But the seventh day is a Sabbath to GOD, your God. Don't do any work—not you, nor your son, nor your daughter, nor your servant, nor your maid, nor your animals, not even the foreign guest visiting in your town. For in six days GOD made Heaven, Earth, and sea, and everything in them; he rested on the seventh day. Therefore GOD blessed the Sabbath day; he set it apart as a holy day. (MSG)

We're not rejecting God; we just don't have time for him. . . . We don't feel guilty because of sin, but because we have no time for our spouses, our children, or our God. It's not sinning too much that's killing our souls, it's our schedule that's annihilating us. Most of us don't come home at night staggering drunk. Instead, we come home staggering tired, worn out, exhausted, and drained because we live too fast.[3]

Mike Yaconelli

Rest was made for us as a gift, so enjoy it.

> Mark 2:27–28 Then Jesus said, "The Sabbath was made to serve us; we weren't made to serve the Sabbath. The Son of Man is no lackey to the Sabbath. He's in charge!" (MSG)

James 1:17 Every good and perfect gift is from above, coming down from the Father of the heavenly lights, who does not change like shifting shadows. (NIV)

· ·

The rest of God . . . is not a reward for finishing. It's not a bonus for work well-done. It's sheer gift. It is a stop-work order in the midst of work that's never complete. . . . Sabbath is not the break we're allotted at the tail end of completing all our tasks and chores. . . . It's the rest we take smack-dab in the middle of them, without apology, without guilt, and for no better reason than God told us we could.[4]

Mark Buchanan

· ·

Trust the Lord of rest.

John 14:1 Don't let your hearts be troubled. Trust in God, and trust also in me. (NLT)

 Psalm 33:4–5 For the word of the Lord holds true, and we can trust everything he does. He loves whatever is just and good; the unfailing love of the Lord fills the earth. (NLT)

PRACTICAL LIVING
· · · · · · · · · · ·

- Choose one day a week to pause from your normal routine. Do things on this day that fill you up—help you to flourish and grow. Delight in what's good. Choose things that enrich.

- What are the things that are draining you? Actively choose times to turn off your computer, your phone, and your TV, to pause your email, etc. Be an active participant in *rest*.

- Choose times to follow Jesus's examples of rest in Matthew 12, and use your day of rest to love and serve others. You may find that a habit of serving others fills you, rather than depletes you.
- Make a practice of resting with your family. Pause from your normal routine. What helps to make your family flourish?
- Create routines that remind you of the Lord of Rest. Begin your day with rest: pray as you wake—trust that God will be working for your good, and his, throughout your day. End your day with rest: pray before you sleep—trust that God will care for you as your body rests.
- Write this on a notecard and keep it as a visual reminder: "I can rest from my unfinished work because the Suffering Servant, Jesus, the Lord of the Sabbath, the Master Rest, declared with his dying breath: *it is finished!*"[5]
- See related topics: Time Management, Work, and Trust.

RECOMMENDED READING

- *Present Over Perfect*. Shauna Niequist. Zondervan.
- *Crazy Busy*. Kevin DeYoung. Crossway.
- *What's Best Next*. Matt Perman. Zondervan.
- *When Work and Family Collide*. Andy Stanley. Multnomah.
- *The Rest of God*. Mark Buchanan. Thomas Nelson.

· Self-Worth ·

The Christian Gospel is that I am so flawed that Jesus had to die for me, yet I am so loved and valued that Jesus was glad to die for me. This leads to deep humility and deep confidence at the same time. It undermines both swaggering and sniveling. I cannot feel superior to anyone, and yet I have nothing to prove to anyone. I do not think more of myself nor less of myself. Instead, I think of myself less.[1]

Tim Keller

Self-worth comes from knowing God.

 Philippians 3:8–9 Yes, everything else is worthless when compared with the infinite value of knowing Christ Jesus my Lord. For his sake I have discarded everything else, counting it all as garbage, so that I could gain Christ and become one with him. I no longer count on my own righteousness through obeying the law; rather, I become righteous through faith in Christ. For God's way of making us right with himself depends on faith. (NLT)

We have self-worth because we are made in God's image.

Genesis 1:26–27 Then God said, "Let us make man in our image, after our likeness." . . . So God created man in his own image, in the image of God he created him; male and female he created them. (ESV)

Our self-worth comes from God's love for us.

Psalm 139:17–18 How precious to me are your thoughts, O God! How vast is the sum of them! If I would count them, they are more than the sand. I awake, and I am still with you. (ESV)

1 John 4:10 This is love: not that we loved God, but that he loved us and sent his Son as an atoning sacrifice for our sins. (NIV)

Our significance is based on our relationship to God, not on any personal qualities and achievements.

Ephesians 2:10 For we are his workmanship, created in Christ Jesus for good works, which God prepared beforehand, that we should walk in them. (ESV)

2 Corinthians 5:17 Therefore, if anyone is in Christ, he is a new creation. The old has passed away; behold, the new has come. (ESV)

Micah 6:8 He has told you, O man, what is good; and what does the LORD require of you but to do justice, and to love kindness, and to walk humbly with your God? (ESV)

PRACTICAL LIVING

- Identify some lies you believe about yourself, and find the truth in Scripture that responds to those lies.
- Memorize Psalm 139:13–16. What does God think about how you are made? Are you useful to him?
- Write on a card, "Knowing God makes life meaningful." Meditate on making that statement true in your life.

RECOMMENDED READING

- *The Freedom of Self-Forgetfulness*. Tim Keller. Penguin.
- *Christ Esteem*. Don Matzat. Harvest House.
- *How to Find Selfless Joy in a Me-First World*. Leslie Vernick. WaterBrook.
- *Free at Last*. Tony Evans. Moody.
- "Women, Trade Self-Worth for Awe and Wonder." Jen Wilkin. (Available online at DesiringGod.org.)
- *Lies Women Believe and the Truth That Sets Them Free*. Nancy Leigh DeMoss. Moody.

· Trials ·

The Garden of Eden was a perfect world——and someday heaven will be perfect. However, we live in the "middle." We live in a broken world—sin, shame, pain, hurt, death, and grief. If it wasn't for God's rescue in Jesus, life and death would not be bearable. But because Jesus conquered death on the cross, we have assurance that he will make all things new.

Suffering and trials are to be expected.

1 Peter 4:12–13 Dear friends, don't be surprised at the fiery trials you are going through, as if something strange were happening to you. Instead, be very glad—for these trials make you partners

with Christ in his suffering, so that you will have the wonderful joy of seeing his glory when it is revealed to all the world. (NLT)

John 16:33 I have said these things to you, that in me you may have peace. In the world you will have tribulation. But take heart; I have overcome the world. (ESV)

God's presence in our suffering is guaranteed.

Isaiah 43:1–2 But now, thus says the LORD, your Creator, O Jacob, and He who formed you, O Israel, "Do not fear, for I have redeemed you; I have called you by name; you are Mine! When you pass through the waters, I will be with you; And through the rivers, they will not overflow you. When you walk through the fire, you will not be scorched, nor will the flame burn you." (NASB)

Psalm 56:8 You keep track of all my sorrows. You have collected all my tears in your bottle. You have recorded each one in your book. (NLT)

. . . .

Suffering is unbearable if you aren't certain that God is for you and with you. . . . Jesus took away the only kind of suffering that can really destroy you: that is being cast away from God. He took that so that now all suffering that comes into your life will only make you great. A lump of coal under pressure becomes a diamond. And the suffering of a person in Christ only turns you into somebody gorgeous.[1]

Tim Keller

. . . .

Trials can develop and improve our character.

 1 Peter 1:6–7 In this you greatly rejoice, even though now for a little while, if necessary, you have been distressed by various trials, so that the proof of your faith, being more precious than gold which

is perishable, even though tested by fire, may be found to result in praise and glory and honor at the revelation of Jesus Christ. (NASB)

James 1:2–5 Consider it pure joy, my brothers and sisters, whenever you face trials of many kinds, because you know that the testing of your faith produces perseverance. Let perseverance finish its work so that you may be mature and complete, not lacking anything. If any of you lacks wisdom, you should ask God, who gives generously to all without finding fault, and it will be given to you. (NIV)

Sometimes suffering comes as the natural result of our flawed, sinful choices, for which we need to repent.

Proverbs 3:11–12 My child, don't reject the LORD's discipline, and don't be upset when he corrects you. For the LORD corrects those he loves, just as a father corrects a child in whom he delights. (NLT)

Hebrews 12:5–7, 10–11 And have you forgotten the exhortation that addresses you as sons? "My son, do not regard lightly the discipline of the Lord, nor be weary when reproved by him. For the Lord disciplines the one he loves, and chastises every son whom he receives." It is for discipline that you have to endure. God is treating you as sons. For what son is there whom his father does not discipline? . . . For they disciplined us for a short time as it seemed best to them, but he disciplines us for our good, that we may share his holiness. For the moment all discipline seems painful rather than pleasant, but later it yields the peaceful fruit of righteousness to those who have been trained by it. (ESV)

Trials help us have soft hearts to encourage others.

2 Corinthians 1:3–5 God is our merciful Father and the source of all comfort. He comforts us in all our troubles so that we can comfort others. When they are troubled, we will be able to give

58

He Giveth More Grace

He giveth more grace when the burdens grow
    greater,
He sendeth more strength when the labors
    increase;
To added affliction He addeth His Mercy,
To multiplied trials, His multiplied peace.

His love has no limit, His grace has no
    measure,
His power no boundary known unto men;
For out of His infinite riches in Jesus
He giveth, and giveth, and giveth again.[2]

Annie Johnson Flint

them the same comfort God has given us. For the more we suffer for Christ, the more God will shower us with his comfort through Christ. (NLT)

Suffering reminds us of Jesus's suffering for us.

1 Peter 4:12–13 Dear friends, don't be surprised at the fiery trials you are going through, as if something strange were happening to you. Instead, be very glad—for these trials make you partners with Christ in his suffering, so that you will have the wonderful joy of seeing his glory when it is revealed to all the world. (NLT)

PRACTICAL LIVING

- Write Isaiah 43:1–2 on a card. (Put your name where it says "Jacob" and "Israel.") Read it each evening.
- Spend time in the Psalms where the authors themselves experienced great trials. Start with these Psalms: 13; 34; 46; 55; 73; 91; 121; 143; and 145.
- How does sharing in Christ's suffering (1 Peter 4:12–13) apply to your current situation?
- Read Romans 8:28–29 and write out a past event in your life that God has used for good.
- Look for ways your experience of suffering can encourage others.
- Memorize James 1:2–5.
- Research God's persecuted church in the Middle East. Pray for those who are suffering.

RECOMMENDED READING

- *A Shelter in the Time of Storm*. Paul Tripp. Crossway.
- *When Life and Beliefs Collide*. Carolyn James. Zondervan.
- *How to Live Right When Your Life Goes Wrong*. Leslie Vernick. WaterBrook.
- *When I Lay My Isaac Down*. Carol Kent. NavPress.
- *A Path Through Suffering*. Elisabeth Elliot. Regal.
- *Trusting God*. Jerry Bridges. NavPress.
- *The Gospel of Ruth*. Carolyn Custis James. Zondervan.
- *Suffering and the Heart of God*. Diane Langberg. New Growth.

· Trust ·

God is the only one we can truly put our trust in. We can depend on him with any matter, at any time—he is always trustworthy.

Trust is to be placed ultimately in God alone.

Psalm 91:1–2 He who dwells in the secret place of the Most High shall abide under the shadow of the Almighty. I will say of the LORD, "He is my refuge and my fortress; My God, in Him I will trust." (NKJV)

John 14:1 Don't let your hearts be troubled. Trust in God, and trust also in me. (NLT)

We are to be wary of trusting ourselves or others.

Psalm 49:12–13 People, despite their wealth, do not endure; they are like the beasts that perish. This is the fate of those who trust in themselves, and of their followers, who approve their sayings. (NIV)

Psalm 118: 8–9 It is better to trust in the LORD than to depend on people. It is better to trust in the LORD than to depend on human leaders. (GNT)

We can trust God in every situation and at every time.

Isaiah 26:4 Trust in the LORD forever, for the LORD GOD is an everlasting rock. (ESV)

Psalm 33:4–5 For the word of the LORD holds true, and we can trust everything he does. He loves whatever is just and good; the unfailing love of the LORD fills the earth. (NLT)

It is as if God were saying "What I am is all that need matter to you, for there lie your hope and your peace. I will do what I will do, and it will all come to light at last, but how I do it is My secret. Trust Me, and be not afraid." With the goodness of God to desire our highest welfare, the wisdom of God to plan it, and the power of God to achieve it, what do we lack? Surely we are the most favored of all creatures.[1]

A. W. Tozer

Trusting in God gives guidance for decisions and plans.

Proverbs 3:5–6 Trust in the LORD with all your heart, and do not lean on your own understanding. In all your ways acknowledge him, and he will make straight your paths. (ESV)

 Psalm 37:3–6 Trust in the LORD and do good; dwell in the land and enjoy safe pasture. Take delight in the LORD, and he will give you the desires of your heart. Commit your way to the LORD; trust in him and he will do this: He will make your righteous reward shine like the dawn, your vindication like the noonday sun. (NIV)

Trust in God to flourish.

Jeremiah 17:5, 7–8 This is what the LORD says: "Cursed are those who put their trust in mere humans, who rely on human strength and turn their hearts away from the LORD. . . . But blessed are those who trust in the LORD and have made the LORD their hope and confidence. They are like trees planted along a riverbank, with roots that reach deep into the water. Such trees are not bothered by the heat or worried by long months of drought. Their leaves stay green, and they never stop producing fruit." (NLT)

Benefits of Trusting God

Protection (Proverbs 30:5)
Gladness (Psalm 64:10)
Peace (Isaiah 26:3)
Blessing (Jeremiah 17:7)
Confidence (Psalm 112:7)

Trust God when fear comes.

Psalm 56:3–4, 11 When I am afraid, I put my trust in you. In God, whose word I praise, in God I trust; I shall not be afraid. What can flesh do to me? . . . in God I trust; I shall not be afraid. What can man do to me? (ESV)

PRACTICAL LIVING

- Study the list of God's names in Appendix C. Each has a meaning that helps us know the God we trust.
- Apply Psalm 63:8 to your life.
- Memorize Proverbs 3:5–6.
- Get some Scrabble letters or letter magnets. Spell "TRUST" and similar words of encouragement. Put the words where you will see them often.
- Set up a bird feeder in your yard. Keep Matthew 6:26–33 in your thoughts as you reflect on God's care for these birds.
- Make a list of the things in your life you're trying to control. How does trust in God affect that list?

RECOMMENDED READING

- *Trusting God*. Jerry Bridges. NavPress.
- *The Attributes of God*. A. W. Tozer. Christian Publications.
- *When God Doesn't Fix It*. Laura Story. Thomas Nelson.
- *The Broken Way*. Ann Voskamp. Zondervan.

Lifestyle

Clothing

Decision Making

Entertainment

Money

Social Media

Time Management

Work

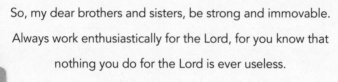

So, my dear brothers and sisters, be strong and immovable. Always work enthusiastically for the Lord, for you know that nothing you do for the Lord is ever useless.

1 Corinthians 15:58 NLT

· Clothing ·

Conversations about clothing, our bodies, and modesty can often highlight shame and temptation. The word *modesty* can sound stifling—we might automatically think of rules, regulations, and restrictions. Because of this, *modesty* evokes poor connotations for many, myself included. But modesty in its true form is quite biblical and it's definitely not tied to shame. An explanation of modesty is twofold: First, it's about finding our identity not in our appearance but in the transforming grace of Christ—we have far more to offer society and our communities than just our bodies. Second, modesty is about preserving and cultivating what God has made precious and beautiful.[1]

Our inner character is far more valuable than our physical appearance.

1 Peter 3:4 But let your adorning be the hidden person of the heart with the imperishable beauty of a gentle and quiet spirit, which in God's sight is very precious. (ESV)

1 Timothy 2:9–10 And I want women to be modest in their appearance. They should wear decent and appropriate clothing and not draw attention to themselves by the way they fix their hair or by wearing gold or pearls or expensive clothes. For women who claim to be devoted to God should make themselves attractive by the good things they do. (NLT)

Will you grab people's attention with hair and jewelry and sexy clothes or will your presence in the room be unmistakable because of your Christlike character? Immodest dress tells the world, "I'm not sure I have anything more to offer than this. What you see is really all you get."[2]

Kevin DeYoung

Tying our worth to outward beauty is dangerous.

Proverbs 31:30 Charm is deceptive, and beauty does not last; but a woman who fears the LORD will be greatly praised. (NLT)

2 Corinthians 4:16–18 For this reason we never become discouraged. Even though our physical being is gradually decaying, yet our spiritual being is renewed day after day. And this small and temporary trouble we suffer will bring us a tremendous and eternal glory, much greater than the trouble. For we fix our attention, not on things that are seen, but on things that are unseen. What can be seen lasts only for a time, but what cannot be seen lasts forever. (GNT)

The modest woman is the woman who deliberately steps back from "the line" of immodesty. This does not mean she wears unattractive, unstylish clothing, but it does mean she's preoccupied with loving God and serving others rather than pushing the limits of immodesty.[3]

Carolyn Mahaney and Nicole Whitacre

God is an artist. Look around; no one is better at cultivating outward beauty. There's nothing inherently wrong with a beautiful appearance or artistic outward expression through clothing.

Psalm 19:1–4 The heavens proclaim the glory of God. The skies display his craftsmanship. Day after day they continue to speak; night after night they make him known. They speak without a sound or word; their voice is never heard. Yet their message has gone throughout the earth, and their words to all the world. (NLT)

Psalm 8:1, 3–4 O Lord, our Lord, your majestic name fills the earth! Your glory is higher than the heavens. . . . When I look at the night sky and see the work of your fingers—the moon and the stars you set in place—what are mere mortals that you should think about them, human beings that you should care for them? (NLT)

God evaluates the heart.

1 Samuel 16:7 The Lord does not look at the things people look at. People look at the outward appearance, but the Lord looks at the heart. (NIV)

1 Corinthians 6:20 For you were bought with a price. So glorify God in your body. (ESV)

Our identity isn't wrapped up in the approval or envy or lust of others. Our identity is found in Christ's life, death and resurrection. Christ is our life. He loved us and refrained from showing off so that we could be His and freed from the need to prove that we've got a great body or wardrobe . . . because we've been lavished with His love instead.[4]

Elyse Fitzpatrick

Modesty guards the precious and intimate.

Song of Solomon 2:7 Promise me, O women of Jerusalem, by the gazelles and wild deer, not to awaken love until the time is right. (NLT)

2 Timothy 2:22 Run from anything that stimulates youthful lusts. Instead, pursue righteous living, faithfulness, love, and peace. Enjoy the companionship of those who call on the Lord with pure hearts. (NLT)

The Bible's call to modesty is not based on the supposed naughtiness of the female form. God's good command to cover up is not meant to punish, but to protect.[5]

Kevin DeYoung

God will take care of your need for clothes.

 Matthew 6:28–30 And why worry about your clothing? Look at the lilies of the field and how they grow. They don't work or make their clothing, yet Solomon in all his glory was not dressed as beautifully as they are. And if God cares so wonderfully for wild-flowers that are here today and thrown into the fire tomorrow, he will certainly care for you. Why do you have so little faith? (NLT)

PRACTICAL LIVING

- Evaluate your clothes. What story do they tell about what you value? Do they protect what is intimate? Seek the advice of a trusted friend or mentor.
- No one cares more about beauty than God. Google pictures of God's creation, the animals he's made, the colors he uses—the things he's made only for beauty's sake.

- Evaluate your motives for clothing purchases—what do you hope to gain by wearing this article of clothing?
- Study Colossians 3, where Paul teaches concerning our new calling in Christ.

RECOMMENDED READING

- *The Lost Art of True Beauty*. Leslie Ludy. Harvest House.
- *True Beauty*. Carolyn Mahaney and Nicole Whitacre. Crossway.
- "Modesty, Objectivism, and Human Value." Richard Poupard. (Available online at Equip.org.)
- "The Lost Virtue of Modesty." Kevin DeYoung. (Available online at TheGospelCoalition.org.)

· Decision Making ·

Simply put, God's will is your growth in Christlikeness. God never assures us of health, success, or ease. But he promises something even better: He promises to make us loving, pure, and humble like Christ. . . . The only chains God wants us to wear are the chains of righteousness—not the chains of hopeless subjectivism, not the shackles of risk-free living, not the fetters of horoscope decision making—just the chains befitting a bondservant of Christ Jesus. Die to self. Live for Christ. And then do what you want, and go where you want, for God's glory.[1]

Kevin DeYoung

71

Have confidence—God has a plan.

Isaiah 42:16 I will lead the blind by a way they do not know, in paths they do not know I will guide them. I will make darkness into light before them and rugged places into plains. These are the things I will do, and I will not leave them undone. (NASB)

Jeremiah 29:11 "For I know the plans that I have for you," declares the LORD, "plans for welfare and not for calamity to give you a future and a hope." (NASB)

Psalm 138:8 The LORD will vindicate me; your love, LORD, endures forever—do not abandon the works of your hands. (NIV)

Determining God's will for your life requires personal prayer, as well as others praying for you.

Colossians 1:9–11 We have not ceased to pray for you and to ask that you may be filled with the knowledge of His will in all spiritual wisdom and understanding, so that you will walk in a manner worthy of the Lord, to please Him in all respects, bearing fruit in every good work and increasing in the knowledge of God; strengthened with all power, according to His glorious might, for the attaining of all steadfastness and patience. (NASB)

 James 1:5 If any of you lacks wisdom, you should ask God, who gives generously to all without finding fault, and it will be given to you. (NIV)

Determining God's will includes seeking the advice of wise believers.

Proverbs 11:14 Where there is no guidance, a people falls, but in an abundance of counselors there is safety. (ESV)

Proverbs 15:22 Without counsel plans fail, but with many advisers they succeed. (ESV)

A willing heart is required to determine the will of God.

Psalm 40:8 I desire to do your will, my God; your law is within my heart. (NIV)

Proverbs 3:5–6 Trust in the LORD with all your heart and do not lean on your own understanding. In all your ways acknowledge Him, and He will make your paths straight. (NASB)

Psalm 37:4–5 Delight yourself in the LORD, and he will give you the desires of your heart. Commit your way to the LORD; trust in him, and he will act. (ESV)

Jeremiah 6:16 This is what the LORD says: "Stop at the crossroads and look around. Ask for the old, godly way, and walk in it. Travel its path, and you will find rest for your souls." (NLT)

Choosing not to sin is always the will of God.

Ephesians 5:15–17 Be very careful, then, how you live—not as unwise but as wise, making the most of every opportunity, because the days are evil. Therefore do not be foolish, but understand what the Lord's will is. (NIV)

2 Timothy 2:22 Flee the evil desires of youth and pursue righteousness, faith, love and peace, along with those who call on the Lord out of a pure heart. (NIV)

Never make a decision that goes against the Word of God.

Deuteronomy 5:29 Oh that they had such a heart in them, that they would fear Me and keep all My commandments always, that it may be well with them and with their sons forever! (NASB)

Psalm 25:4–5 Show me your ways, LORD, teach me your paths. Guide me in your truth and teach me, for you are God my Savior, and my hope is in you all day long. (NIV)

PRACTICAL LIVING

. . . .

- Gain perspective before making a decision. Seek out a trusted Christian leader (pastor, mentor, or counselor). Explain your situation and the decisions that need to be made. Ask for advice.
- Write out the choices you must make and evaluate them according to Scripture.
- Spend time in fasting, prayer, and meditation. Pray for wisdom and discernment.
- Involve trusted, wise friends who will counsel and pray for you.
- Ask yourself if your decision will bring glory to God.
- Take time. Do not rush. Wait on God.
- See Appendix D for more information on decision making.

RECOMMENDED READING

. . . .

- *Just Do Something: A Liberating Approach to Finding God's Will*. Kevin DeYoung. Moody.
- *What's Best Next: How the Gospel Transforms the Way You Get Things Done*. Matt Perman. Zondervan.
- *Decision Making and the Will of God*. Garry Friesen. Multnomah.
- *God's Will: Guidance for Everyday Decisions*. J. I. Packer. Baker.
- *God's Guidance*. Elisabeth Elliot. Revell.

· Entertainment ·

The best of art, culture, and entertainment tell a true story. Whether Christian or secular, fiction or nonfiction, happy or sad—*good* art tells a *true* story. How do we determine a true story from one that tells lies? We look for echoes—for similarities between the stories we watch, read, and listen to and the ultimate true story in the Bible. We use discernment and wisdom about the thoughts, ideas, and pictures we put into our minds and hearts.

True stories, in themselves, may look extremely different. Some stories highlight darkness and tell of the depraved nature of man, where all is not as it ought to be. Sometimes, a story that speaks truth centers on light, beauty, and joy and reflects the peace of a happy ending. What's important is that both stories are telling an important truth about this world God created—fallenness and redemption. The most dangerous entertainment lies about the consequences of poor decisions, unrealistic expectations, human nature, etc. These are the stories, the distortions of truth, that we must most carefully guard ourselves against.

The best art always allows us to come in, to see something of ourselves, to know something about ourselves that we would not be able to see or know otherwise.[1]

Steven Garber

When God created mankind in his image, he included his creativity and love for beauty. We express that image through creative cultural representations.

Psalm 8:1, 3–4 O LORD, our Lord, how majestic is your name in all the earth! You have set your glory above the heavens. . . . When I look at your heavens, the work of your fingers, the moon and the stars, which you have set in place, what is man that you are mindful of him, and the son of man that you care for him? (ESV)

Genesis 1:27, 31 So God created man in his own image, in the image of God he created him; male and female he created them. . . . And God saw everything that he had made, and behold, it was very good. And there was evening and there was morning, the sixth day. (ESV)

We must actively pursue what is right, making careful, godly decisions.

Colossians 3:2–5 Set your minds on things that are above, not on things that are on earth. For you have died, and your life is hidden with Christ in God. When Christ who is your life appears, then you also will appear with him in glory. Put to death therefore what is earthly in you: sexual immorality, impurity, passion, evil desire, and covetousness, which is idolatry. (ESV)

Colossians 2:6 And now, just as you accepted Christ Jesus as your Lord, you must continue to follow him. (NLT)

 Romans 12:2 Don't copy the behavior and customs of this world, but let God transform you into a new person by changing the way you think. Then you will learn to know God's will for you, which is good and pleasing and perfect. (NLT)

One more time, Walker Percy was right: Bad books always lie; they lie most of all about the human condition. And bad art of every kind always lies, missing the meaning of who we are—just as good art tells the truth about the human condition.[2]

Steven Garber

Satan attempts to corrupt and degrade all that God has created for good, including our cultural expressions, by replacing them with counterfeits.

John 8:44 [Satan] has always hated the truth, because there is no truth in him. When he lies, it is consistent with his character; for he is a liar and the father of lies. (NLT)

1 John 5:19 We know that we are of God, and that the whole world lies in the power of the evil one. (NASB)

We must diligently recognize the corruptions of Satan—they are false representations and distortions of the truth.

3 John 11 Beloved, do not imitate what is evil, but what is good. The one who does good is of God; the one who does evil has not seen God. (NASB)

Psalm 101:3–4 I will not look with approval on anything that is vile. I hate what faithless people do; I will have no part in it. The perverse of heart shall be far from me; I will have nothing to do with what is evil. (NIV)

Galatians 5:19–21 The acts of the flesh are obvious: sexual immorality, impurity and debauchery; idolatry and witchcraft; hatred, discord, jealousy, fits of rage, selfish ambition, dissensions, factions and envy; drunkenness, orgies, and the like. I warn you, as I did before, that those who live like this will not inherit the kingdom of God. (NIV)

Colossians 2:8 See to it that no one takes you captive through hollow and deceptive philosophy, which depends on human tradition and the elemental spiritual forces of this world rather than on Christ. (NIV)

At the heart of our faith is the bold claim that in a world full of stories, with a world's worth of heroes, villains, comedies, tragedies, twists of fate, and surprise endings, there is really only one story. One grand narrative [God as creator, Jesus as rescuer] subsumes and encompasses all the other comings and goings of every creature—real or fictitious—on the earth.[3]

Mike Cosper

Choose entertainment carefully; pursue truth and not the world's distortions.

Isaiah 5:20 Woe to those who call evil good and good evil, who put darkness for light and light for darkness, who put bitter for sweet and sweet for bitter. (NIV)

Psalm 101:2–3 I will be careful to live a blameless life—when will you come to help me? I will lead a life of integrity in my own home. I will refuse to look at anything vile and vulgar. I hate all who deal crookedly; I will have nothing to do with them. (NLT)

2 Timothy 2:22 Run from anything that stimulates youthful lusts. Instead, pursue righteous living, faithfulness, love, and peace. Enjoy the companionship of those who call on the Lord with pure hearts. (NLT)

Think on this: God's artistic choices should govern our own. More than any other type of artist, Christian artists should be truth-lovers and truth-tellers. More than any other consumer,

Christian readers—and parents of young readers—should be truth-seekers.[4]

N. D. Wilson

PRACTICAL LIVING

- Practice thinking critically about the movies and TV shows you watch. Do they tell the truth about life? Or do they leave you with unrealistic expectations? Do they accurately portray the consequences of bad decisions?
- Research movies before viewing. Don't be caught unaware by harmful or destructive content.
- Try practicing family dinners around a table. Turn off the TV during meals.

RECOMMENDED READING

- *The Stories We Tell: How TV and Movies Long for and Echo the Truth*. Mike Cosper. Crossway.
- *The Christian Imagination: The Practice of Faith in Literature and Writing*. Leland Ryken. WaterBrook Press.
- *From the Garden to the City: The Redeeming and Corrupting Power of Technology*. John Dyer. Kregel Publications.
- *The Social Church: A Theology of Digital Communication*. Justin Wise. Moody.

· Money ·

When my husband told me he thought we should attend Financial Peace University, a biblically based finance management class taught by author Dave Ramsey, I (Rachel) had the absolute worst attitude. I almost cried on the way to our first class, and you can believe I complained the entire way. We were about to have our second child, and I was in the midst of designing and purchasing things for the nursery—no one was going to tell me I couldn't have the nursery I wanted. In short, I was miserable, my husband was miserable, and our finances were miserable. But then something happened. Somewhere in between making and *following* a budget for the first time in my life and hearing Dave Ramsey personally chastise me (that's what it felt like), my heart changed. I realized that I was foolish—not only were my financial decisions and lack of financial planning hurting me, they were hurting my husband (a dear and amazingly patient man) and my children. I was so clearly living outside of God's plan for my life, a plan that he's put into place for my benefit and health. God's given us the tools to live a financially secure, productive, and generous life—and I was making sure I squandered these gifts at every opportunity. But there was a better way!

God has provided us with the knowledge and wisdom to live a financially wise life. Don't squander these gifts.

Matthew 7:24–27 Anyone who listens to my teaching and follows it is wise, like a person who builds a house on solid rock. Though the rain comes in torrents and the floodwaters rise and the winds beat against that house, it won't collapse because it is built on bedrock. But anyone who hears my teaching and doesn't obey it is foolish, like a person who builds a house on sand. When the rains and floods come and the winds beat against that house, it will collapse with a mighty crash. (NLT)

Proverbs 21:20 The wise store up choice food and olive oil, but fools gulp theirs down. (NIV)

Proverbs 21:5 Good planning and hard work lead to prosperity, but hasty shortcuts lead to poverty. (NLT)

A budget is people telling their money where to go instead of wondering where it went.[1]

John Maxwell

Ultimately, everything belongs to God. It is only by his provision we have anything.

1 Chronicles 29:11–12 Yours, O LORD, is the greatness and the power and the glory and the victory and the majesty, for all that is in the heavens and in the earth is yours. Yours is the kingdom, O LORD, and you are exalted as head above all. Both riches and honor come from you, and you rule over all. In your hand are power and might, and in your hand it is to make great and to give strength to all. (ESV)

Deuteronomy 8:18 And you shall remember the LORD your God, for it is He who gives you power to get wealth, that He may establish His covenant which He swore to your fathers, as it is this day. (NKJV)

One of the dangers of having a lot of money is that you may be quite satisfied with the kinds of happiness money can give and so fail to realize your need for God. If everything seems to come simply by signing checks, you may forget that you are at every moment totally dependent on God.[2]

C. S. Lewis

We must choose what will be our priority—God or money.

Matthew 6:24 No one can serve two masters. Either he will hate the one and love the other, or he will be devoted to the one and despise the other. You cannot serve both God and money. (NIV)

 Hebrews 13:5 Keep your lives free from the love of money and be content with what you have, because God has said, "Never will I leave you; never will I forsake you." (NIV)

· ·

Money can buy fun, but not happiness.[3]
Dave Ramsey

· ·

Live contentedly. Guard your heart against greed and jealousy.

1 Timothy 6:17 As for the rich in this present age, charge them not to be haughty, nor to set their hopes on the uncertainty of riches, but on God, who richly provides us with everything to enjoy. (ESV)

Proverbs 15:16 Better is a little with the fear of the Lord than great treasure and trouble with it. (ESV)

1 Timothy 6:9–10 Those who want to get rich fall into temptation and a trap and into many foolish and harmful desires that plunge people into ruin and destruction. For the love of money is a root of all kinds of evil. Some people, eager for money, have wandered from the faith and pierced themselves with many griefs. (NIV)

Matthew 6:19–21 Do not store up for yourselves treasures on earth, where moth and rust destroy, and where thieves break in and steal. But store up for yourselves treasures in heaven, where neither moth nor rust destroys, and where thieves do not break in or steal; for where your treasure is, there your heart will be also. (NASB)

One definition of maturity is learning to delay pleasure. Children do what feels good; adults devise a plan and follow it.[4]

Dave Ramsey

Part of our income needs to be given back to God.

Proverbs 3:9–10 Honor the LORD with your possessions, and with the first fruits of all your increase; so your barns will be filled with plenty, and your vats will overflow with new wine. (NKJV)

2 Corinthians 9:7 Each one must give as he has decided in his heart, not reluctantly or under compulsion, for God loves a cheerful giver. (ESV)

Live generously.

Proverbs 11:25 The generous will prosper; those who refresh others will themselves be refreshed. (NLT)

Gain all you can, save all you can, give all you can.[5]

John Wesley

Debt to the government and others must be paid.

Romans 13:6–8 This is also why you pay taxes, for the authorities are God's servants, who give their full time to governing. Give to everyone what you owe them: If you owe taxes, pay taxes; if revenue, then revenue; if respect, then respect; if honor, then honor. Let no debt remain outstanding, except the continuing debt to love one another, for whoever loves others has fulfilled the law. (NIV)

PRACTICAL LIVING

- Sign up for a Financial Peace University course.
- Always tithe first. Then save. Then buy.
- If your credit card use is out of control, stop using them. Cut them up and pay them off.
- Maintain a budget plan with financial goals. Plan for purchases.
- Seek out trusted, wise organizations in need of financial help. Give generously!

RECOMMENDED READING

- *Sex and Money*. Paul David Tripp. Crossway.
- *Counterfeit Gods*. Tim Keller. Penguin.
- *Money, Possessions and Eternity*. Randy Alcorn. Tyndale.
- *Debt-Free Living*. Larry Burkett. Moody.
- *Total Money Makeover*. Dave Ramsey. Thomas Nelson.

· Social Media ·

In our culture, there are few easier ways to waste time, feel inadequate, lose contentment, and receive approval or rejection than through social media. Social media is a powerful tool for both businesses and entertainment in our lives. It is in no way inherently bad, but it's definitely not safe. Its use should be treated and evaluated with care, integrity, and as always, through the lens of Scripture.

Love God's creation, not man's imperfect systems.

 1 John 2:15–16 Do not love the world or the things in the world. If anyone loves the world, the love of the Father is not in him. For all that is in the world—the desires of the flesh and the desires of the eyes and pride of life—is not from the Father but is from the world. (ESV)

As Christians we believe that what happens in our minds is integral to what happens in our souls. . . . Because social media engages our minds and emotions, we have a Christian obligation to evaluate whether we engage to our benefit or to our stumbling.[1]

Samuel James

Make good use of your time. Set time limits and stick to them.

Ephesians 5:15–17 Look carefully then how you walk, not as unwise but as wise, making the best use of the time, because the days are evil. Therefore do not be foolish, but understand what the will of the Lord is. (ESV)

Seek contentment with circumstances and possessions.

Hebrews 13:5 Keep your life free from love of money, and be content with what you have, for he has said, "I will never leave you nor forsake you." (ESV)

Psalm 37:7, 16 Be patient and wait for the LORD to act; don't be worried about those who prosper or those who succeed in their evil plans. . . . The little that a good person owns is worth more than the wealth of all the wicked. (GNT)

Pursue and view what is good.

> Psalm 119:37 Turn my eyes from looking at worthless things; and give me life in your ways. (ESV)

> Psalm 101:3–4 I will not look with approval on anything that is vile. I hate what faithless people do; I will have no part in it. The perverse of heart shall be far from me; I will have nothing to do with what is evil. (NIV)

Gossiping is always wrong.

> Proverbs 20:19 A gossip betrays a confidence; so avoid anyone who talks too much. (NIV)

. . . .

Navigating the pleasures and perils of social media requires wisdom, reflection, and a life lived in close proximity to the means of grace God has ordained for his church. . . . Unplugging can be helpful, but even more helpful than unplugging from the Internet is plugging into the truth of God's Word, the beauty of God's world, and the community of God's people.[2]

Samuel James

. . . .

Any boasting must be in God, not self. Find value and validation through integrity—a life well lived, not social media.

> Jeremiah 9:23–24 This is what the LORD says: "Let not the wise boast of their wisdom or the strong boast of their strength or the rich boast of their riches, but let the one who boasts boast about this: that they have the understanding to know me, that I am the LORD, who exercises kindness, justice and righteousness on earth, for in these I delight," declares the LORD. (NIV)

Don't use social media to stir up trouble.

Ephesians 4:31 Let all bitterness and wrath and anger and clamor and slander be put away from you, along with all malice. (ESV)

PRACTICAL LIVING

- Consider taking a break from social media. What aspects of your life does this break change or affect, if any? Are you more content? More or less connected with the people around you?
- Read the article, "The Pleasures and Perils of the Online Life" by Samuel James (available online at TheGospelCoalition. org). Write down a few things you found helpful or were encouraged to change.
- For one week, write down how much time you spend on the computer. Total these hours and consider what you have accomplished with this time.
- Beware of the types of relationships you are building online. Do they honor the boundaries God has put in place? Are they emotionally healthy?
- How much time are you spending "talking" with people you have never met? Is too much time spent keeping you from meaningful contact with family and friends?

RECOMMENDED READING

- *Reclaiming Conversation: The Power of Talk in a Digital Age.* Sherry Turkle. Penguin.
- "10 Ways the Church Needs to Rethink its Social Media Usage." Krish Kandiah. *Christian Today* (website).

- *The Social Church: A Theology of Digital Communication.* Justin Wise. Moody.
- *Hope & Help for Video Game, TV, and Internet "Addiction"* (booklet). Mark Shaw. Focus.

· Time Management ·

Productivity is an issue that affects all of us every day. Who hasn't been overwhelmed with email, frustrated they reached the end of the day without completing anything on their to-do list, or procrastinated yet again on starting that important task? There are lots of good strategies and tips out there for managing ourselves better. But there's one thing we often overlook: what does God have to say about getting things done and being productive? This is an important question because, as Christians, we are to think about all areas of life—not just some—from a biblical perspective.[1]

Matt Perman

God desires that we use our time wisely.

Psalm 90:12 So teach us to number our days that we may gain a heart of wisdom. (NKJV)

 Ephesians 5:15–17 So be careful how you live. Don't live like fools, but like those who are wise. Make the most of every opportunity in these evil days. Don't act thoughtlessly, but understand what the Lord wants you to do. (NLT)

1 Corinthians 14:40 But everything should be done in a fitting and orderly way. (NIV)

. . . .

How we spend our days is, of course, how we spend our lives.[2]

Annie Dillard

. . . .

God does not just consider our actions, but also our motives.

Colossians 3:17 Whatever you do in word or deed, do all in the name of the Lord Jesus, giving thanks through Him to God the Father. (NASB)

Romans 14:12 So then each of us will give an account of himself to God. (ESV)

1 Corinthians 15:58 So, my dear brothers and sisters, be strong and immovable. Always work enthusiastically for the Lord, for you know that nothing you do for the Lord is ever useless. (NLT)

Our work should be our best.

Ecclesiastes 9:10 Whatever you do, do well. For when you go to the grave, there will be no work or planning or knowledge or wisdom. (NLT)

. . . .

Aimless, unproductive Christians contradict the creative, purposeful, powerful, merciful God we love.[3]

John Piper

. . . .

89

Completion of a job well done is not only based on skill, but also on God's blessing.

Psalm 90:17 Let the favor of the LORD our God be upon us; and confirm for us the work of our hands; yes, confirm the work of our hands. (NASB)

Staying balanced is crucial for time management.

Ecclesiastes 7:18 Whoever fears God will avoid all extremes. (NIV)

Delegation of responsibilities is a biblical concept.

Exodus 18:18, 21–22 You're going to wear yourself out—and the people, too. This job is too heavy a burden for you to handle all by yourself. . . . But select from all the people some capable, honest men who fear God and hate bribes. Appoint them as leaders over groups of one thousand, one hundred, fifty, and ten. They should always be available to solve the people's common disputes, but have them bring the major cases to you. Let the leaders decide the smaller matters themselves. They will help you carry the load, making the task easier for you. (NLT)

PRACTICAL LIVING

- Read Matt Perman's essay "The Key to Gospel-Driven Productivity" (available online at TheGospelCoalition.org). Spend time thinking and journaling about how this changes your views on productivity.
- Use a planner or app on your phone to keep a detailed schedule. Review it. Stick to it.
- Keep a visual family calendar.

- Brainstorm things that could hurt your productivity. Keep a tally of time spent on these things. Should you make any changes?
- See related topics: Work and Rest.

RECOMMENDED READING

- *What's Best Next: How the Gospel Transforms the Way You Get Things Done*. Matthew Perman. Zondervan.
- *Work Matters*. Tom Nelson. Crossway.
- *Getting Things Done*. David Allen. Penguin.
- *When Work and Family Collide*. Andy Stanley. Multnomah.
- *The Get Yourself Organized Project*. Kathi Lipp. Harvest House.

· Work ·

We were created by God to work, whether in an office, in the home, or in a field—God has made us to create, design, contribute, heal, clean, plant, and countless other tasks and jobs. Whether unpaid, seen, or unseen—work is a part of God's plan for each of us. God's intention is that we work to ultimately serve him, and by extension, our communities, our churches, our companies, and our families—and in doing so, we can find fulfillment in good work well done.

God's plan for work was established at the very beginning.

> Genesis 2:15 The LORD God took the man and put him in the garden of Eden to work it and keep it. (ESV)

- -

Christians shouldn't be known as the people who get donuts for the meeting and then stink at their jobs; we should be known as the people so excellent at our jobs that we don't only excel in our work, we help others excel in theirs too.[1]

Matt Perman

- -

Whatever our work—it is of great value to God.

> Colossians 3:17 Whatever you do in word or deed, do all in the name of the Lord Jesus, giving thanks through Him to God the Father. (NASB)

> Colossians 3:23–25 Work willingly at whatever you do, as though you were working for the Lord rather than for people. Remember that the Lord will give you an inheritance as your reward, and that the Master you are serving is Christ. But if you do what is wrong, you will be paid back for the wrong you have done. For God has no favorites. (NLT)

- -

The only Christian work, is good work well done.[2]

Dorothy Sayers

- -

Work is about serving God.

> 2 Corinthians 5:20 We are ambassadors for Christ, God making his appeal through us. (ESV)

The quality, integrity, and ethics of our work matter.

> Jeremiah 17:10 But I, the LORD, search all hearts and examine secret motives. I give all people their due rewards, according to what their actions deserve. (NLT)

> Ecclesiastes 12:13–14 Fear God and obey his commands, for this is everyone's duty. God will judge us for everything we do, including every secret thing, whether good or bad. (NLT)

The Church's approach to an intelligent carpenter is usually confined to exhorting him not to be drunk and disorderly in his leisure hours, and to come to church on Sundays. What the Church should be telling him is this: that the very first demand that his religion makes upon him is that he should make good tables.[3]

Dorothy Sayers

Work is not about serving ourselves, but about serving others.

> Philippians 2:3–4 Do nothing from selfish ambition or conceit, but in humility count others more significant than yourselves. Let each of you look not only to his own interests, but also to the interests of others. (ESV)

> 1 Peter 4:10 As each has received a gift, use it to serve one another, as good stewards of God's varied grace. (ESV)

Thinking of work mainly as a means of self-fulfillment and self-realization slowly crushes a person.[4]

Tim Keller

93

Balance is crucial. Resting in God helps work to flourish.

Genesis 2:2 And on the seventh day God finished his work that he had done, and he rested on the seventh day from all his work that he had done. (ESV)

Hebrews 4:10 For whoever has entered God's rest has also rested from his works as God did from his. (ESV)

John 15:4 Abide in me, and I in you. As the branch cannot bear fruit by itself, unless it abides in the vine, neither can you, unless you abide in me. (ESV)

PRACTICAL LIVING

- Get involved in various internships or volunteer work to get a sense of how you are gifted and what you enjoy.
- Write down what types of work bring you joy. How can you use these things to help and bring joy to others?
- Evaluate the work you do—its quality, ethics, and morals. Is it bringing glory to God? Is it helping others? Do changes need to be made?
- Make a list of the difficult or distasteful aspects of your work. How does the fact that your work matters to God change your perspective?
- See related topics: Rest and Time Management.

RECOMMENDED READING

- *A Woman's Place: A Christian Vision for Your Calling in the Office, the Home, and the World.* Katelyn Beaty. Howard Books.
- *What's Best Next: How the Gospel Transforms the Way You Get Things Done.* Matthew Perman. Zondervan.

- *Work Matters*. Tom Nelson. Crossway.
- *The Call: Finding and Fulfilling the Central Purpose of Your Life*. Os Guinness. Thomas Nelson.
- *Every Good Endeavor*. Tim Keller. Penguin.
- *Present Over Perfect*. Shauna Niequist. Zondervan.
- *When Work and Family Collide*. Andy Stanley. Multnomah.

Daily Struggles

Bitterness

Depression

Difficult Memories

Disappointment

Grief

Guilt

Loneliness

Pride

Worry

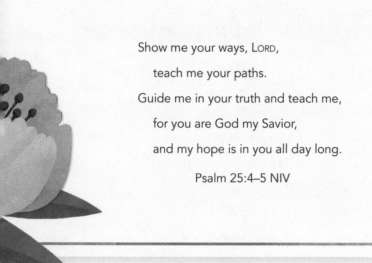

Show me your ways, Lord,

teach me your paths.

Guide me in your truth and teach me,

for you are God my Savior,

and my hope is in you all day long.

Psalm 25:4–5 NIV

· Bitterness ·

Unchecked in a person's life, bitterness becomes like a spiritual cancer. It will eat away and destroy a person's life. It is the result of an unwillingness to forgive when we have been wronged, hurt, or mistreated—it enables us to hang on to our hurt and keep it close in our lives.

Bitterness damages our lives and relationships.

Hebrews 12:15 See to it that no one comes short of the grace of God; that no root of bitterness springing up causes trouble, and by it many be defiled. (NASB)

James 3:14–16 But if in your heart you are jealous, bitter, and selfish, don't sin against the truth by boasting of your wisdom. Such wisdom does not come down from heaven; it belongs to the world, it is unspiritual and demonic. Where there is jealousy and selfishness, there is also disorder and every kind of evil. (GNT)

Bitterness is characteristic of someone who does not believe the gospel.

James 3:10–12 Words of thanksgiving and cursing pour out from the same mouth. My friends, this should not happen! No spring of water pours out sweet water and bitter water from the same opening. A fig tree, my friends, cannot bear olives; a grapevine cannot bear figs, nor can a salty spring produce sweet water. (GNT)

Acts 8:23 For I see that you are full of bitterness and captive to sin. (NIV)

Forgive, because Christ has forgiven you.

 Ephesians 4:31–32 Get rid of all bitterness, rage, anger, harsh words, and slander, as well as all types of evil behavior. Instead, be kind to each other, tenderhearted, forgiving one another, just as God through Christ has forgiven you. (NLT)

Trust God; he is sovereign and has a perfect plan.

Psalm 37:1 Don't be worried on account of the wicked; don't be jealous of those who do wrong. (GNT)

Romans 12:17–19 Repay no one evil for evil, but give thought to do what is honorable in the sight of all. If possible, so far as it depends on you, live peaceably with all. Beloved, never avenge yourselves, but leave it to the wrath of God, for it is written, "Vengeance is mine, I will repay, says the Lord." (ESV)

Avoid anger, which leads to bitterness. Don't be known as an angry person.

James 1:19–20 My dear brothers and sisters, take note of this: Everyone should be quick to listen, slow to speak and slow to become angry, because human anger does not produce the righteousness that God desires. (NIV)

Proverbs 14:17 People with a hot temper do foolish things; wiser people remain calm. (GNT)

. . . .

We fool ourselves into thinking no one will know, but anger and resentment have a way of seeping into everything. Resentment is like a beach ball we try to submerge in the water. No matter how valiant our efforts, it pops up with all its vitality, splashing everyone around.[1]

Anne Peterson

. . . .

PRACTICAL LIVING

- Write about what makes you bitter. Talk to God about the injustice you feel. Construct steps to move toward forgiveness and freedom.
- Study Matthew 18:21–35. What steps do you need to take to move toward forgiveness and a life free of bitterness?
- Commit to pray for those who have hurt you.
- Memorize Ephesians 4:31–32.
- Pray for God to soften your heart so you are willing to give up your bitterness.
- See related topics: Forgiving Others, Sin and God's Forgiveness.

RECOMMENDED READING

- "Four Ways to Battle Bitterness." Jen Wilkin. (Available online at TheGospelCoalition.org.)
- *Overcoming Emotions That Destroy*. Chip Ingram. Baker.
- *Good and Angry*. David Powlison. New Growth Press.
- *When You've Been Wronged*. Erwin Lutzer. Moody.
- *You Can Change*. Tim Chester. Crossway.

· Depression ·

Depression can feel like a burden too heavy to bear. It is real, painful, and exhausting. With such a large variety of possible emotional, physical, spiritual, and mental causes it can feel like a mountain too tall to climb. But even if you have lost hope, you are not alone. You can depend on God and his Word through this season. You can depend on the people God has brought into your life to help you. If you feel like you are alone, please seek a qualified person to help—a physician, counselor, or trusted friend. Do not suffer in silence or alone. God is totally dependable. You are not alone. God's people are never alone, even in the darkest moments. There's nothing you feel, nothing you think, nothing you've gone through that takes God by surprise. Nothing can separate you from the love of God (Romans 8:39).

I (Pat) found myself in this unfamiliar pit. I thought I would never smile again, that my children would never have a happy mom. I needed hope! For me, hope came in the truth of God and his character. Rather than become immobile, I had to push toward hope and God's unchanging promises. The time seemed long, the road unimaginable, the work of believing truth a minute-by-minute fight. I had to take care of my health, repent where necessary, and grab onto God's Word like a starving prisoner. This passage was instrumental in pushing me toward freedom:

Isaiah 43:18–19 Forget the former things; do not dwell on the past. See, I am doing a new thing! Now it springs up; do you not perceive it? I am making a way in the wilderness and streams in the wasteland. (NIV)

Depression is a journey, but you will not stay there forever. God used it to help me grow, soften my heart, and help me to conform to the image of his Son (Romans 8:29). Live in hope, dear one. Live in hope.

> Psalm 27:7–9 Listen, GOD, I'm calling at the top of my lungs: "Be good to me! Answer me!" When my heart whispered, "Seek God," my whole being replied, "I'm seeking him!" Don't hide from me now! You've always been right there for me; don't turn your back on me now. Don't throw me out, don't abandon me; you've always kept the door open. (MSG)

Depression is an overwhelming burden that causes despair.

> Proverbs 18:14 The human spirit can endure a sick body, but who can bear a crushed spirit? (NLT)

> Psalm 6:6–7 I am weary with my moaning; every night I flood my bed with tears; I drench my couch with my weeping. My eye wastes away because of grief; it grows weak because of all my foes. (ESV)

> Psalm 5:1–3 Listen to my words, LORD, consider my lament. Hear my cry for help, my King and my God, for to you I pray. In the morning, LORD, you hear my voice; in the morning I lay my requests before you and wait expectantly. (NIV)

God knows and understands your despair.

> Psalm 38:9 O Lord, all my longing is before you; my sighing is not hidden from you. (ESV)

> Psalm 9:12 God remembers those who suffer; he does not forget their cry. (GNT)

God has not forgotten you.

> Psalm 37:23–24 The LORD directs the steps of the godly. He delights in every detail of their lives. Though they stumble, they will never fall, for the LORD holds them by the hand. (NLT)

2 Corinthians 4:16 Therefore we do not lose heart. Though outwardly we are wasting away, yet inwardly we are being renewed day by day. (NIV)

Seek God's protection during this hard time.

Psalm 69:13–15 But I keep praying to you, Lord, hoping this time you will show me favor. In your unfailing love, O God, answer my prayer with your sure salvation. Rescue me from the mud; don't let me sink any deeper! Save me from those who hate me, and pull me from these deep waters. Don't let the floods overwhelm me, or the deep waters swallow me, or the pit of death devour me. (NLT)

God is not threatened or surprised by your dark thoughts.

Psalm 88:15–18 From my youth I have suffered and been close to death; I have borne your terrors and am in despair. Your wrath has swept over me; your terrors have destroyed me. All day long they surround me like a flood; they have completely engulfed me. You have taken from me friend and neighbor—darkness is my closest friend. (NIV)

There is hope in God.

 Psalm 43:5 Why are you in despair, O my soul? And why are you disturbed within me? Hope in God, for I shall again praise Him, the help of my countenance and my God. (NASB)

Psalm 16:8 I have set the Lord always before me; because he is at my right hand, I shall not be shaken. (ESV)

Psalm 73:25–26 Whom have I in heaven but You? And besides You, I desire nothing on earth. My flesh and my heart may fail, but God is the strength of my heart and my portion forever. (NASB)

The hope we have in Jesus forces us to look at such frightening trials differently. All of God's promises to His people are confirmed to be real and true *because Jesus was resurrected*. If the greatest enemy (death) has been defeated, then all lesser enemies (fires, injuries, illnesses, victimization, etc.) must be no match for the Lord.[1]

Jeff Forrey

A part of moving out of depression is evaluating our emotions. Are we allowing emotions to direct our behavior?

Philippians 4:6–8 Don't worry about anything; instead, pray about everything. Tell God what you need, and thank him for all he has done. Then you will experience God's peace, which exceeds anything we can understand. His peace will guard your hearts and minds as you live in Christ Jesus. And now, dear brothers and sisters, one final thing. Fix your thoughts on what is true, and honorable, and right, and pure, and lovely, and admirable. Think about things that are excellent and worthy of praise. (NLT)

Jeremiah 29:11–12 For I know the plans I have for you, declares the LORD, plans for welfare and not for evil, to give you a future and a hope. Then you will call upon me and come and pray to me, and I will hear you. (ESV)

Disobedience to God can lead to depression.

Genesis 4:6–7 Then the LORD said to Cain, "Why are you angry? Why is your face downcast? If you do what is right, will you not be accepted? But if you do not do what is right, sin is crouching at your door; it desires to have you, but you must rule over it." (NIV)

When sin is the cause of depression, repentance and confession must take place for the depression to lift.

Psalm 32:3–5 When I refused to confess my sin, my body wasted away, and I groaned all day long. Day and night your hand of discipline was heavy on me. My strength evaporated like water in the summer heat. Finally, I confessed all my sins to you and stopped trying to hide my guilt. I said to myself, "I will confess my rebellion to the LORD." And you forgave me! All my guilt is gone. (NLT)

PRACTICAL LIVING

- See a wise, trusted counselor.
- See your physician for a physical. Ask about blood tests for vitamin D, vitamin B12, thyroid, etc.
- Begin an exercise regimen. Plan for thirty minutes at least three times a week. Begin by walking.
- Monitor your sleeping habits. Are you getting enough sleep? Ironically, some depressed people sleep too much and need to cut themselves back to eight hours.
- Consider volunteering at your church, or a food pantry or homeless shelter. You are needed, you are valuable, and you can help others.
- Make a list of lies you are believing; contrast these with the truth of Scripture.
- Track depressed days, looking for patterns or hormonal swings. Record what triggers you toward sadness. A certain time of day? A specific place?
- Read daily Psalms 27 and 37.
- Share struggles with strong believers who can provide objectivity.
- Evaluate: Are you choosing or holding onto sinful patterns? In need of repentance?
- See related topics: Hope, Trials, Trust, and Worry.

RECOMMENDED READING

- *Depression: A Stubborn Darkness.* Ed Welch. New Growth Press.
- *Seeing Depression Through the Eyes of Grace.* Julie Ganschow. PureWater Press.
- *Will Medicine Stop the Pain?* Elyse Fitzpatrick and Laura Hendrickson. Moody.
- *When the Darkness Will Not Lift.* John Piper. Crossway.
- *Getting Over the Blues: A Woman's Guide to Fighting Depression.* Leslie Vernick. Harvest House.
- *Walking With God Through Pain and Suffering.* Tim Keller. Penguin.

· Difficult Memories ·

Hard memories can destroy. They can color our joy. Steal happy moments. Rob us of peace and sleep. Difficult memories are as wide and as varied as we are as people; each experience is different, filled with circumstances we made for ourselves, and worse, situations that were chosen for us. Whether you are dealing with memories as a result of your own choices and the guilt and regret that follows, or with memories that were forced on you by destructive and sinful people—you are not alone. God offers solace and comfort. He offers forgiveness when necessary. He offers protection and defense from memories beyond our control. He offers justice for those who have hurt us. He offers comfort for the grieving. No matter what you remember, God offers hope. You are not alone.

God offers solace and comfort.

Psalm 31:1–3 In you, O LORD, do I take refuge; let me never be put to shame; in your righteousness deliver me! Incline your ear to me; rescue me speedily! Be a rock of refuge for me, a strong fortress to save me! For you are my rock and my fortress; and for your name's sake you lead me and guide me. (ESV)

God offers forgiveness.

Psalm 130:3–4 If you, LORD, kept a record of sins, Lord, who could stand? But with you there is forgiveness, so that we can, with reverence, serve you. (NIV)

God offers protection and defense from memories beyond our control.

Isaiah 43:18–19 Remember not the former things, nor consider the things of old. Behold, I am doing a new thing; now it springs forth, do you not perceive it? I will make a way in the wilderness and rivers in the desert. (ESV)

God offers justice for those who have hurt us.

Matthew 10:26 But don't be afraid of those who threaten you. For the time is coming when everything that is covered will be revealed, and all that is secret will be made known to all. (NLT)

God offers comfort for the grieving.

Psalm 28:7 The Lord is my strength and my shield; My heart trusted in Him, and I am helped; Therefore my heart greatly rejoices, And with my song I will praise Him. (NKJV)

No matter what you remember, God offers hope.

Psalm 62:5–6 For God alone, O my soul, wait in silence, for my hope is from him. He only is my rock and my salvation, my fortress; I shall not be shaken. (ESV)

Concentrate on what God is doing in the present and will do in the future.

Isaiah 26:3–4 You will keep in perfect peace all who trust in you, all whose thoughts are fixed on you! Trust in the Lord always, for the Lord God is the eternal Rock. (NLT)

2 Corinthians 5:17 Therefore, if anyone is in Christ, he is a new creation; old things have passed away; behold, all things have become new. (NKJV)

Quit being paralyzed by your past. Grace offers you life in the present and guarantee of a future.[1]

Paul Tripp

Past mistakes, losses, and wounds can trap us, limiting our ability to enjoy the present or future.

Philippians 3:13–15 Brothers, I do not consider that I have made it my own. But one thing I do: forgetting what lies behind and straining forward to what lies ahead, I press on toward the goal for the prize of the upward call of God in Christ Jesus. (ESV)

Ephesians 4:22–24 You were taught, with regard to your former way of life, to put off your old self, which is being corrupted by its deceitful desires; to be made new in the attitude of your minds; and to put on the new self, created to be like God in true righteousness and holiness. (NIV)

The battle of dealing with the past takes place in the mind.

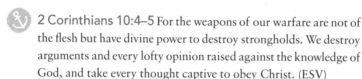 2 Corinthians 10:4–5 For the weapons of our warfare are not of the flesh but have divine power to destroy strongholds. We destroy arguments and every lofty opinion raised against the knowledge of God, and take every thought captive to obey Christ. (ESV)

Philippians 4:8 Summing it all up, friends, I'd say you'll do best by filling your minds and meditating on things true, noble, reputable, authentic, compelling, gracious—the best, not the worst; the beautiful, not the ugly; things to praise, not things to curse. (MSG)

If past memories involve sin, be sure that repentance and confession have taken place.

1 John 1:9 But if we confess our sins to him, he is faithful and just to forgive us our sins and to cleanse us from all wickedness. (NLT)

Psalm 32:1–5 Oh, what joy for those whose disobedience is forgiven, whose sin is put out of sight! Yes, what joy for those whose record the LORD has cleared of guilt, whose lives are lived in complete honesty! When I refused to confess my sin, my body wasted away, and I groaned all day long. Day and night your hand of discipline was heavy on me. My strength evaporated like water in the summer heat. Finally, I confessed all my sins to you and stopped trying to hide my guilt. I said to myself, "I will confess my rebellion to the LORD." And you forgave me! All my guilt is gone. (NLT)

Focus on God's provision for the past.

Psalm 25:6–7 Remember, O LORD, Your tender mercies and Your lovingkindnesses, for they are from of old. Do not remember the sins of my youth, nor my transgressions; According to Your mercy remember me, for Your goodness' sake, O LORD. (NKJV)

Psalm 77:11 I shall remember the deeds of the LORD; surely I will remember Your wonders of old. (NASB)

PRACTICAL LIVING

- Make a record of God's goodness, provision, and providence. Continue to focus on this throughout life with gratitude and thanksgiving. Cry out to God (see Psalm 88). Give yourself time to grieve difficult memories. Freedom, especially when trauma is involved, is a process.
- If others have sinned against you, make sure you have forgiven them. Often, forgiveness is a difficult journey, especially when grievous wrongs have been committed against us. Study forgiveness, thank God for his own forgiveness of you, and pray that he will help change your heart and help you to forgive others. Forgiveness is often a process, as well as a choice.
- Prayerfully examine your heart. Consider what past memories are coming to your mind repeatedly. Journal what you value as you dwell on these memories. What do you fear?
- Study the Psalms, especially Psalm 88 and Psalm 25. What does God understand about your past? What hope does he offer you within these painful memories?
- See related topics: Forgiving Others, Grief, Trials, Hope, Self-Worth, and the Knowing God section.

RECOMMENDED READING

- *Walking with God through Pain and Suffering*. Tim Keller. Penguin.
- *Prodigal God*. Tim Keller. Penguin.
- *Putting the Past Behind You*. Erwin Lutzer. Moody.
- *Putting Your Past in Its Place*. Steve Viars. Harvest House.
- "How Can I Get Over the Guilt of Past Sexual Sin?" in *Intimate Issues*. Linda Dillow. WaterBrook.
- *One Thousand Gifts: A Dare to Live Fully Right Where You Are*. Ann Voskamp. Zondervan.

· Disappointment ·

Every disappointing day reminds us that this is not our home. When the days don't go our way, we long for a better life, where there are no more tears, disappointments, sorrows, and suffering. A life where the God who faithfully promised to keep us to the end will wipe every tear of disappointment away forever.[1]

Courtney Reissig

God knows and cares about the brokenhearted.

Psalm 56:8 You keep track of all my sorrows. You have collected all my tears in your bottle. You have recorded each one in your book. (NLT)

Job 23:8–10 Behold, I go forward but He is not there, and backward, but I cannot perceive Him; when He acts on the left, I cannot behold Him; He turns on the right, I cannot see Him. But He knows the way I take; when He has tried me, I shall come forth as gold. (NASB)

God will provide relief from disappointment. He is the only one who can truly meet our needs.

Psalm 34:18 The LORD is near to the brokenhearted and saves those who are crushed in spirit. (NASB)

Psalm 147:3 He heals the brokenhearted and binds up their wounds. (NASB)

Ecclesiastes 3:11 Yet God has made everything beautiful for its own time. He has planted eternity in the human heart, but even so, people cannot see the whole scope of God's work from beginning to end. (NLT)

 John 14:1, 27 Don't let your hearts be troubled. Trust in God, and trust also in me. . . . I am leaving you with a gift—peace of mind and heart. And the peace I give is a gift the world cannot give. So don't be troubled or afraid. (NLT)

God is in charge of the events of our lives and only allows what is for our ultimate good.

Jeremiah 29:11–13 "For I know the plans I have for you," says the LORD. "They are plans for good and not for disaster, to give you a future and a hope. In those days when you pray, I will listen. If you look for me wholeheartedly, you will find me." (NLT)

James 1:2–5 Dear brothers and sisters, when troubles of any kind come your way, consider it an opportunity for great joy. For you know that when your faith is tested, your endurance has a chance to grow. So let it grow, for when your endurance is fully developed, you will be perfect and complete, needing nothing. If you need wisdom, ask our generous God, and he will give it to you. He will not rebuke you for asking. (NLT)

. . . .

God is not in the business of "making the best of it" when things don't go our way. He doesn't just sweep in and pick up the pieces after our best-laid plans fall apart. He is always working, even in our disappointments, and using those trials for a greater purpose.[2]

Courtney Reissig

. . . .

God encourages believers to bear one another's burdens.

Galatians 6:2 Carry each other's burdens, and in this way you will fulfill the law of Christ. (NIV)

Do not let Satan use disappointment to defeat you.

1 Peter 5:8–9 Stay alert! Watch out for your great enemy, the devil. He prowls around like a roaring lion, looking for someone to devour. Stand firm against him, and be strong in your faith. Remember that your family of believers all over the world is going through the same kind of suffering you are. (NLT)

God can use our disappointments to help others who are hurting.

2 Corinthians 1:3–4 Let us give thanks to the God and Father of our Lord Jesus Christ, the merciful Father, the God from whom all help comes! He helps us in all our troubles, so that we are able to help others who have all kinds of troubles, using the same help that we ourselves have received from God. (GNT)

Today is a gift. And if we have tomorrow, tomorrow will be a gift. It's rebellious in a way, to choose to love your life. It's much easier, and much more common to be miserable. But I choose to do what I can do to create hope, to celebrate life, and the act of celebrating connects me back to that life that I love.[3]

Shauna Niequist

PRACTICAL LIVING

- Even amidst the darkest disappointment, find something to celebrate—even the smallest beauty or victory.
- Look at the characteristics of God listed in Appendix A. Which are the ones you tend to doubt?
- Memorize Psalm 34:18 and Psalm 147:3.

RECOMMENDED READING

- *One Thousand Gifts: A Dare to Live Fully Right Where You Are*. Ann Voskamp. Zondervan.
- *When I Lay My Isaac Down*. Carol Kent. NavPress.
- *Bittersweet*. Shauna Niequist. Zondervan.
- *When Your World Falls Apart*. David Jeremiah. Thomas Nelson.
- *Fear, Worry and the God of Rest*. Ed Welch. New Growth.
- *God's Healing for Life's Losses*. Robert W. Kellemen. BMH Books.
- *When God Doesn't Fix It*. Laura Story. Thomas Nelson.

· Grief ·

Amy Balentine reflects on her grief two years after the death of her son Simon:

> I am so thankful for this grief—truly—it seems weird to say, but I am. I'm finding that if you want to see Jesus and the Holy Spirit move, you have got to draw near to the brokenhearted. So many people say, "God is good!" when a baby is born, a promotion at work is received, or new house is bought. And it's true. He IS good in those times. But we hardly hear, "God is good!" when a baby is lost, a father is laid off of his job or a house burns to the ground. No, in these times, we say . . . where are you God? It might seem wrong and a bit inappropriate to say, "God is good" in a time of deep grief. But I can attest, he is good and can often be seen and felt more when the times are bad. If we can allow ourselves to fall into his arms, he'll wrap us up in his arms, carry us and stand us back up.[1]

God offers comfort when grief overwhelms. He has not left us alone.

Psalm 28:7 The LORD is my strength and my shield; my heart trusted in Him, and I am helped; therefore my heart greatly rejoices, and with my song I will praise Him. (NKJV)

Psalm 30:5 His favor is for life; weeping may endure for a night, but joy comes in the morning. (NKJV)

Isaiah 43:2 When you pass through the waters, I will be with you; and through the rivers, they shall not overflow you. When you walk through the fire, you shall not be burned, nor shall the flame scorch you. (NKJV)

God, in his goodness, is our refuge in grief.

 Psalm 31:1–3 In you, O LORD, do I take refuge; let me never be put to shame; in your righteousness deliver me! Incline your ear to me; rescue me speedily! Be a rock of refuge for me, a strong fortress to save me! For you are my rock and my fortress; and for your name's sake you lead me and guide me. (ESV)

Psalm 31:9 Be gracious to me, O LORD, for I am in distress; my eye is wasted from grief; my soul and my body also. (ESV)

Joy can be found in the midst of grief.

Psalm 126:5–6 Those who plant in tears will harvest with shouts of joy. They weep as they go to plant their seed, but they sing as they return with the harvest. (NLT)

Isaiah 55:12 [My word] shall not return to me empty, but it shall accomplish that which I purpose, and shall succeed in the thing for which I sent it. For you shall go out in joy and be led forth in peace; the mountains and the hills before you shall break forth into singing and all the trees of the field shall clap their hands. (ESV)

Jesus, the Man of Sorrows, understands our grief.

Isaiah 53:3 He was despised and rejected by men; a man of sorrows and acquainted with grief; and as one from whom men hide their faces he was despised, and we esteemed him not. (ESV)

Isaiah 53:5–6 But he was pierced for our transgressions; he was crushed for our iniquities; upon him was the chastisement that brought us peace, and with his wounds we are healed. All we like sheep have gone astray; we have turned—every one—to his own way; and the LORD has laid on him the iniquity of us all. (ESV)

Luke 22:41–44 And he withdrew from them about a stone's throw, and knelt down and prayed, saying, "Father, if you are willing, remove this cup from me. Nevertheless, not my will, but yours, be done." And there appeared to him an angel from heaven, strengthening him. And being in agony he prayed more earnestly; and his sweat became like great drops of blood falling down to the ground. (ESV)

. . . .

Jesus Christ suffered, not so that we would never suffer but so that when we suffer we would be like him. His suffering led to glory. . . . And if you know that glory is coming, you can handle suffering too.[2]

Tim Keller

. . . .

Knowing God's control of future events comforts us in our grief.

Isaiah 55:8–9 For my thoughts are not your thoughts, neither are your ways my ways, declares the LORD. For as the heavens are higher than the earth, so are my ways higher than your ways and my thoughts than your thoughts. (ESV)

1 Thessalonians 4:13 Our friends, we want you to know the truth about those who have died, so that you will not be sad, as are those who have no hope. (GNT)

Psalm 116:15 Precious in the sight of the LORD is the death of his saints. (ESV)

PRACTICAL LIVING

- Spend time in the Psalms, especially 32; 34; 37; 42; 46; 91; and 145.
- Listen to the sermon "Praying our Tears" by Tim Keller (available online at GospelInLife.com).
- Schedule specific times to express your grief. Allow yourself to cry and pour your heart out to God.
- Join a gospel-centered support group to help you in your grief (like Grief Share). You are not alone.
- Claim God's sovereignty. Write his attributes on a card, and carry it in your pocket to review daily.
- Be consistent in healthy habits: Bible reading, daily exercise, healthy eating, and meeting with godly encouragers.
- Read Amy Balentine's story (available online at www.balen tinememoirs.com).

RECOMMENDED READING

- *Walking with God through Pain and Suffering*. Tim Keller. Riverhead.
- "The Truth about Grief: What I Wish I Had Known When I Started My Grief Journey." Abby Rike. (Available online at RockThis.org.)
- *Grieving with Hope*. Kathy Leonard. Baker.
- *What Grievers Can Expect*. Wally Stephenson. RBP.
- *When Life Is Changed Forever*. Rick Taylor. Harvest House.

· Guilt ·

Guilt can serve as an excellent, God-given reminder of unforgiven sin and the need for repentance. But for imperfect people living in a tainted world, guilt can also control us and keep us in a constant state of inadequacy. Even the best things we do, even the most selfless, fall short of perfection. We could easily live our entire lives with a feeling of self-loathing and a constant sense of low-lying guilt.

When perfection is the standard, we can always try harder, always do more, and always live less selfishly. But the gospel provides a new way. Christ's death gives us freedom. We shouldn't learn to ignore guilt—it is an excellent indicator of sin. But we also shouldn't live our lives constantly feeling like failures. The gospel frees us from self-righteousness and equally frees us from self-loathing. Through the gospel, we are liberated from guilt.

We need to repent of our sins and seek forgiveness.

1 John 1:8–10 If we say that we have no sin, we are deceiving ourselves and the truth is not in us. If we confess our sins, He is faithful and righteous to forgive us our sins and to cleanse us from all unrighteousness. If we say that we have not sinned, we make Him a liar and His word is not in us. (NASB)

 Hebrews 10:22–23 Let us draw near to God with a sincere heart and with the full assurance that faith brings, having our hearts sprinkled to cleanse us from a guilty conscience and having our bodies washed with pure water. Let us hold unswervingly to the hope we profess, for he who promised is faithful. (NIV)

Live in the grace of the gospel.

Ephesians 2:4–8 But God's mercy is so abundant, and his love for us is so great, that while we were spiritually dead in our disobedience he brought us to life with Christ. It is by God's grace that you have been saved. In our union with Christ Jesus he raised us up with him to rule with him in the heavenly world. He did this to demonstrate for all time to come the extraordinary greatness of his grace in the love he showed us in Christ Jesus. For it is by God's grace that you have been saved through faith. It is not the result of your own efforts, but God's gift, so that no one can boast about it. (GNT)

God is aware of our shame and willing to help.

Psalm 31:17 Do not let me be ashamed, O LORD, for I have called upon You; let the wicked be ashamed; let them be silent in the grave. (NKJV)

Psalm 71:1–3 In You, O LORD, I put my trust; let me never be put to shame. Deliver me in your righteousness, and cause me to escape; incline Your ear to me, and save me. Be my strong refuge, to which I may resort continually; You have given the commandment to save me, for You are my rock and my fortress. (NKJV)

When we repent, God offers true forgiveness.

Isaiah 1:18 "Come now, and let us reason together," says the LORD, "though your sins are as scarlet, they will be as white as snow; though they are red like crimson, they will be like wool." (NASB)

Psalm 103:12 As far as the east is from the west, so far has He removed our transgressions from us. (NASB)

Isaiah 43:25 I, even I, am the one who wipes out your transgressions for my own sake, and I will not remember your sins. (NASB)

If we are truly sinning, we need to repent and implore the Lord to help us change. But if we aren't sinning, if we are perhaps not as mature as we could be, or are not as disciplined as some believers, or we are making different choices that may be acceptable but not extraordinary, then we should not be made to feel guilty. Challenged, stirred, inspired, but not guilty.[1]

Kevin DeYoung

PRACTICAL LIVING

- To help you understand what God has done in forgiveness, write your sins on small rocks and throw them into a lake. Believe he has done what he said in Micah 7:18–20.
- Write down your understanding of why Jesus went to the cross. Do you believe that it was for this sin that he died?
- Understand that if you feel guilty after confessing and repenting, that feeling does not come from God. Study the verses about what God does with confessed, repentant, and forgiven sin in Appendix E.

RECOMMENDED READING

- *The Prodigal God*. Tim Keller. Penguin.
- *Shame Interrupted*. Ed Welch. New Growth.
- *The Gospel for Real Life*. Jerry Bridges. NavPress.

· Loneliness ·

Jesus took the ultimate loneliness upon himself on the cross—separation from God. He became loneliness, so that we never have to experience this sort of separation. Loneliness is real and difficult, but we are never truly alone, never truly alienated, because we have the promise that God is always with us. When Jesus died and paid for our failures and all the things we mess up and get wrong, he ensured that, if we believe, we will never be separated from God.

· ·

The only love that won't disappoint you is one that can't change, that can't be lost, that is not based on the ups and downs of life or of how well you live. It is something that not even death can take away from you. God's love is the only thing like that.[1]

Tim Keller

· ·

The reality of loneliness.

Psalm 38:9–11 O Lord, all my longing is before you; my sighing is not hidden from you. My heart throbs; my strength fails me, and the light of my eyes—it also has gone from me. My friends and companions stand aloof from my plague, and my nearest kin stand far off. (ESV)

Job 19:13–14 He has put my brothers far from me, and those who knew me are wholly estranged from me. My relatives have failed me, my close friends have forgotten me. (ESV)

Psalm 142:1–4 I cry aloud to the LORD; I lift up my voice to the LORD for mercy. I pour out before him my complaint; before him I tell my trouble. When my spirit grows faint within me, it is you who watch over my way. In the path where I walk people have hidden a snare for me. Look and see, there is no one at my right hand; no one is concerned for me. I have no refuge; no one cares for my life. (NIV)

Loneliness is so pervasive, it can even make us feel separated from God.

Job 23:8–9 Behold, I go forward but He is not there, and backward, but I cannot perceive Him; when He acts on the left, I cannot behold Him; He turns on the right, I cannot see Him. (NASB)

Psalm 13:1 How long, O Lord? Will You forget me forever? How long will You hide Your face from me? (NASB)

We can cry out to God in our loneliness.

Psalm 25:16 Turn to me and be gracious to me, for I am lonely and afflicted. (NASB)

 Psalm 62:5–8 I depend on God alone; I put my hope in him. He alone protects and saves me; he is my defender, and I shall never be defeated. My salvation and honor depend on God; he is my strong protector; he is my shelter. Trust in God at all times, my people. Tell him all your troubles, for he is our refuge. (GNT)

. . . .

Loneliness is a wilderness, but through receiving it as a gift, accepting it from the hand of God and offering it back to him with thanksgiving, it may become a pathway to holiness, to glory and to God himself.[2]

Elisabeth Elliot

. . . .

God is always with us—we are never truly alone.

Deuteronomy 31:6 Be strong and of good courage, do not fear nor be afraid of them; for the LORD your God, He is the One who goes with you. He will not leave you nor forsake you. (NKJV)

Joshua 1:9 Have I not commanded you? Be strong and of good courage; do not be afraid, nor be dismayed, for the LORD your God is with you wherever you go. (NKJV)

Jesus experienced the ultimate loneliness on the cross, so that we'll never be truly alone again.

Matthew 27:46 About the ninth hour Jesus cried out with a loud voice, saying, "ELI, ELI, LEMA SABACHTHANI?" that is, "MY GOD, MY GOD, WHY HAVE YOU FORSAKEN ME?" (NASB)

Deuteronomy 31:6 Be strong and courageous. Do not fear or be in dread of them, for it is the LORD your God who goes with you. He will not leave you or forsake you. (ESV)

God will provide for us when we feel alone.

Zephaniah 3:17 The LORD your God in your midst, The Mighty One, will save; He will rejoice over you with gladness, He will quiet you with His love, He will rejoice over you with singing. (NKJV)

Psalm 68:5–6 A father of the fatherless and a judge for the widows, is God in His holy habitation. God makes a home for the lonely; He leads out the prisoners into prosperity, only the rebellious dwell in a parched land. (NASB)

Psalm 73:25–26 Whom have I in heaven but You? And besides You, I desire nothing on earth. My flesh and my heart may fail, but God is the strength of my heart and my portion forever. (NASB)

. . . .

The pain of loneliness arises from the constitution of our nature. God made us for each other. The desire for human companionship is completely natural and right. The loneliness of the Christian results from his walk with God in an ungodly world, a walk that must often take him away from the fellowship of good Christians as well as from that of the unregenerate world.[3]

A. W. Tozer

. . . .

PRACTICAL LIVING

. . . .

- Memorize Deuteronomy 31:6. Write it on a 3x5 card. Put it where you will see it daily.
- Listen to the sermon series "Only the Lonely" by Paul Matthies (available online at TVCResources.net).
- Open your home to the lonely. Read Sarah's story, "How One Woman Created a Community Out of a Neighborhood" (available online at StorylineBlog.com). Even if it's on a much smaller scale, how can you follow her example?
- Actively engage in group activities that will help you draw out of isolation.
- Anticipate places and times of loneliness so you can be prepared. Remind yourself beforehand of God's character and his presence with you.
- Chart out a normal week. How much time are you spending alone? With God? With others? In ministry? Community Service? Work? Relaxing?
- Look for others who may be alone; minister to them.
- Monitor your "self-pity" thinking. Practice Philippians 4:8!
- See related topics: Church, Friendship, and Hospitality.

RECOMMENDED READING

• *Prodigal God*. Tim Keller. Penguin.
• *The Path of Loneliness*. Elisabeth Elliot. Revell.
• *Lonely People*. Warren Wiersbe. Baker.
• *Trusting God When Life Hurts*. Jerry Bridges. NavPress.

· Pride ·

I (Rachel) don't know how many times I've said to our daughter Lucy, "Good job! You should be proud of yourself! You worked so hard!" I'm proud of her. She's proud of her work. We're all feeling very proud of ourselves. And it's right and good to take satisfaction in our work and a job well done. Right for children to work hard at learning a task and to feel accomplished afterwards. But in unhealthy doses, pride can seep into our lives and take control of many areas in our hearts. We've all seen people who are filled with their own self-importance, inflated self-worth, and conceit in their own accomplishments. Or if we're honest, we recognize those feelings in our own hearts—it's painful when I ask myself the question, "Am I genuinely happy and thankful for Lucy's accomplishments, that she's learning and growing? Or am I actually just happy that I think she's learning and growing faster than another child? Am I prideful about her accomplishments simply because they reflect well on me?" Do you see the difference? Am I thanking God for the abilities that God has given my daughter?

Or does conceit and self-worth overwhelm my heart—to the detriment of loving others and Christ well?

. . . .

Pride is taking credit for what God has done. To know that all we have is a gift, that all we experience and enjoy is an expression of God's goodness and not ours, to know that everything in our possession—especially our salvation—comes from the hand of God is to take the first step in defeating and dethroning pride from our hearts.[1]

Sam Storms

. . . .

Pride is an especially dangerous sin.

Proverbs 16:5 Everyone who is arrogant in heart is an abomination to the LORD; be assured, he will not go unpunished. (ESV)

Proverbs 6:16–19 There are six things that the LORD hates, seven that are an abomination to him: haughty eyes, a lying tongue, and hands that shed innocent blood, a heart that devises wicked plans, feet that make haste to run to evil, a false witness who breathes out lies, and one who sows discord among brothers. (ESV)

. . . .

According to Christian teachers, the essential vice, the utmost evil, is Pride. Unchastity, anger, greed, drunkenness, and all that, are mere flea bites in comparison: it was through Pride that the devil became the devil: Pride leads to every other vice: it is the complete anti-God state of mind. . . . [I]t is Pride which has been the chief cause of misery in every nation and every family since the world began.[2]

C. S. Lewis

. . . .

Pride destroys.

Psalm 18:27 You rescue the humble, but you humiliate the proud. (NLT)

Proverbs 13:10 Pride leads to conflict; those who take advice are wise. (NLT)

Proverbs 16:18 Pride goes before destruction, and a haughty spirit before a fall. (NKJV)

Isaiah 2:11 Human pride will be brought down, and human arrogance will be humbled. Only the Lord will be exalted on that day of judgment. (NLT)

. . . .

Pride is the soil in which all manner of sin germinates and grows.[3]

Sam Storms

. . . .

Replace pride with humility.

 Philippians 2:3–4 Don't be selfish; don't try to impress others. Be humble, thinking of others as better than yourselves. Don't look out only for your own interests, but take an interest in others, too. (NLT)

Romans 12:3 For by the grace given me I say to every one of you: Do not think of yourself more highly than you ought, but rather think of yourself with sober judgment, in accordance with the faith God has distributed to each of you. (NIV)

. . . .

Pride is your greatest enemy, humility is your greatest friend.[4]

John Stott

. . . .

God is pleased with humility.

Proverbs 26:12 Do you see a person wise in their own eyes? There is more hope for a fool than for them. (NIV)

Proverbs 21:4 Haughty eyes and a proud heart, the lamp of the wicked, are sin. (ESV)

James 4:6 But He gives more grace. Therefore He says: "God resists the proud, but gives grace to the humble." (NKJV)

. . . .

True gospel-humility means I stop connecting every experience, every conversation, with myself. In fact, I stop thinking about myself.[5]

Tim Keller

. . . .

There is only one boasting that pleases God—praise directed to him.

Jeremiah 9:23–24 GOD's Message: "Don't let the wise brag of their wisdom. Don't let heroes brag of their exploits. Don't let the rich brag of their riches. If you brag, brag of this and this only: That you understand and know me. I'm GOD, and I act in loyal love. I do what's right and set things right and fair, and delight in those who do the same things. These are my trademarks." GOD's Decree. (MSG)

Galatians 6:14 But far be it from me to boast except in the cross of our Lord Jesus Christ, by which the world has been crucified to me, and I to the world. (ESV)

God is the source of all we have and all we do.

John 15:5 I am the vine; you are the branches. Whoever abides in me and I in him, he it is that bears much fruit, for apart from me you can do nothing. (ESV)

1 Timothy 6:17 As for the rich in this present age, charge them not to be haughty, nor to set their hopes on the uncertainty of riches, but on God, who richly provides us with everything to enjoy. (ESV)

PRACTICAL LIVING

- Memorize Philippians 2:3–4. As you review the verses, ask— why do I feel I am always right or better than others?
- Practice "breathing grace" to others. Practice not voicing your pride with one-upmanship, needing to have the last word.
- As you confess pride to God, ask him to reveal your areas of weakness.
- Spend time daily in thanksgiving. Focus on God's gifts of talent, ability, family, financial security. God owns it all; give credit to him.

RECOMMENDED READING

- "The Great Sin" in *Mere Christianity*. C. S. Lewis. HarperOne.
- *The Freedom of Self-Forgetfulness*. Tim Keller. Penguin.
- *From Pride to Humility*. Stuart Scott. Focus.
- *Humility: The Forgotten Virtue*. Wayne Mack. P&R.
- *Respectable Sins*. Jerry Bridges. NavPress.
- "Women, Trade Self-Worth for Awe and Wonder." Jen Wilkin. (Available online at DesiringGod.org.)

· Worry ·

Worry is something that a lot of us live and struggle with daily. The face of this anxiety can change—it acts as a constant whisper in the background and at times as a brief, all-consuming shout. It's such a real part of our lives that we may not even notice that it's our almost constant companion. But the gospel changes everything. Because Jesus already conquered death, we don't need to be consumed by our anxiety. Not all of our fears will be erased, but thankfully, we don't need to live in their shadow. Through Christ, our fear loses its power; it does not need to incapacitate or paralyze us. God knows the dangers of living in a fallen world better than any of us. He gave us the tools and his words to help us live with wisdom and confidence, rather than with the worries that can consume and control us.

Though we live in a fallen world—in which terrorism, robbery, identity theft, rudeness, callousness, deception, etc., are all too common—the resurrection of Jesus changes the way we look at and live in the world.[1]

Jeff Forrey

Worry grabs us when we fail to focus on God's love and care for us, when we fear what "might be" rather than what is real and true.

Job 23:8–9 Behold, I go forward, but he is not there, and backward, but I do not perceive him; on the left hand when he is working,

I do not behold him; he turns to the right hand, but I do not see him. (ESV)

Christ's death and resurrection transform our worry and fears.

Romans 8:38–39 For I am sure that neither death nor life, nor angels nor rulers, nor things present nor things to come, nor powers, nor height nor depth, nor anything else in all creation, will be able to separate us from the love of God in Christ Jesus our Lord. (ESV)

Psalm 73:25–26 Whom have I in heaven but you? I desire you more than anything on earth. My health may fail, and my spirit may grow weak, but God remains the strength of my heart; he is mine forever. (NLT)

1 Peter 1:3 Blessed be the God and Father of our Lord Jesus Christ! According to his great mercy, he has caused us to be born again to a living hope through the resurrection of Jesus Christ from the dead. (ESV)

Do not allow fear to control your mind; instead, focus on what is true and real.

Psalm 33:13–14, 18–19 The Lord looks down from heaven and sees the whole human race. From his throne he observes all who live on the earth. . . . But the Lord watches over those who fear him, those who rely on his unfailing love. He rescues them from death and keeps them alive in times of famine. (NLT)

Philippians 4:8–9 And now, dear brothers and sisters, one final thing. Fix your thoughts on what is true, and honorable, and right, and pure, and lovely, and admirable. Think about things that are excellent and worthy of praise. Keep putting into practice all you learned and received from me—everything you heard from me and saw me doing. Then the God of peace will be with you. (NLT)

The proper response to worry is trusting God with our concerns.

1 Peter 5:7 Give all your worries and cares to God, for he cares about you. (NLT)

 Philippians 4:6–7 Don't worry about anything; instead, pray about everything. Tell God what you need, and thank him for all he has done. Then you will experience God's peace, which exceeds anything we can understand. His peace will guard your hearts and minds as you live in Christ Jesus. (NLT)

Isaiah 41:10 Do not fear, for I am with you; do not anxiously look about you, for I am your God. I will strengthen you, surely I will help you, surely I will uphold you with My righteous right hand. (NASB)

God's sufficient resources are enough for our every concern.

2 Corinthians 12:9 But he said to me, "My grace is sufficient for you, for my power is made perfect in weakness." Therefore I will boast all the more gladly of my weaknesses, so that the power of Christ may rest upon me. (ESV)

Philippians 4:13, 19 I can do all things through him who strengthens me. . . . And my God will supply every need of yours according to his riches in glory in Christ Jesus. (ESV)

Do we believe God is in control? Trust puts anxiety to rest.

Psalm 139:16 Your eyes saw my unformed substance; in your book were written, every one of them, the days that were formed for me, when as yet there were none of them. (ESV)

Isaiah 45:5–7 I am the LORD, and there is no other; apart from me there is no God. I will strengthen you, though you have not acknowledged me, so that from the rising of the sun to the place of its setting people may know there is none besides me. I am the

LORD, and there is no other. I form the light and create darkness,
I bring prosperity and create disaster; I, the LORD, do all these
things. (NIV)

. . . .

As I have struggled with anxiety . . . I have come to the conclu-
sion that my anxiety is triggered not so much by a distrust in
God as by an unwillingness to submit to and cheerfully accept
his agenda for me.[2]

Jerry Bridges

. . . .

Anxiety about the future is sheltered in God's ultimate plan.

Isaiah 26:3–4 You will keep in perfect peace those whose minds
are steadfast, because they trust in you. Trust in the LORD forever,
for the LORD, the LORD himself, is the Rock eternal. (NIV)

A worry problem is really a love problem.

1 John 4:18 There is no fear in love; but perfect love casts out
fear, because fear involves punishment, and the one who fears is
not perfected in love. (NASB)

Jeremiah 31:3 The LORD appeared to him from afar, saying, "I
have loved you with an everlasting love; therefore I have drawn you
with lovingkindness." (NASB)

We don't need to worry about the past.

Isaiah 43:18–19 Remember not the former things, nor consider
the things of old. Behold, I am doing a new thing; now it springs
forth, do you not perceive it? (ESV)

We don't need to worry about the future.

Proverbs 3:5–6 Trust in the LORD with all your heart and do not lean on your own understanding. In all your ways acknowledge Him, and He will make your paths straight. (NASB)

Matthew 6:34 So do not worry about tomorrow; for tomorrow will care for itself. Each day has enough trouble of its own. (NASB)

We can trust God to know what we need for daily life.

Matthew 6:26–27, 31–33 Look at the birds of the air: they neither sow nor reap nor gather into barns, and yet your heavenly Father feeds them. Are you not of more value than they? And which of you by being anxious can add a single hour to his span of life? . . . Therefore do not be anxious, saying, "What shall we eat?" or "What shall we drink?" or "What shall we wear?" For the Gentiles seek after all these things, and your heavenly Father knows that you need them all. But seek first the kingdom of God and his righteousness, and all these things will be added to you. (ESV)

God provides protection.

Psalm 61:1–4 Hear my cry, O God, listen to my prayer; from the end of the earth I call to you when my heart is faint. Lead me to the rock that is higher than I, for you have been my refuge, a strong tower against the enemy. Let me dwell in your tent forever! Let me take refuge under the shelter of your wings! (ESV)

Psalm 91:4 He shall cover you with His feathers, and under His wings you shall take refuge; his truth shall be your shield and buckler. (NKJV)

Psalm 4:8 In peace I will both lie down and sleep, for You alone, O LORD, make me to dwell in safety. (NASB)

PRACTICAL LIVING

- Memorize Isaiah 41:10.
- Read the essay "Why Are You Worried?" by Timothy Lane (available online at TheGospelCoalition.org).
- Pray your fears aloud.
- Journal your fears. Make a list of the ways God shows his love for you.
- Read chapter 22 in the book *The Knowledge of the Holy* by A. W. Tozer.
- Write down your worries, or pray your worries aloud to God—give him your concerns.
- Make a "thankful list" of what God has done to relieve past concerns.
- Set up a bird feeder in your yard. Keep Matthew 6:26–33 in your thoughts as you reflect on God's care for these birds.
- Staying physically active can help with anxiety. Work out at least three days a week for thirty minutes or more.
- Read Psalm 18 aloud daily.
- See related topics: Trust and Hope.

RECOMMENDED READING

- *Calm My Anxious Heart*. Linda Dillow. NavPress.
- *Overcoming Fear, Worry, and Anxiety*. Elyse Fitzpatrick. Harvest House.
- *Anxious for Nothing*. John MacArthur. Victor.
- "Christ, God's Answer to Your Fear" in *Women Counseling Women*. Elyse Fitzpatrick. Harvest House.
- *Living Without Worry*. Timothy Lane. The Good Book Company.

Relationships

Church

Communication

Forgiving Others

Friendship

Hospitality

Marriage

Mothering

Singleness

If you've gotten anything at all out of following Christ, if his love has made any difference in your life, if being in a community of the Spirit means anything to you, if you have a heart, if you care—then do me a favor: Agree with each other, love each other, be deep-spirited friends. Don't push your way to the front; don't sweet-talk your way to the top. Put yourself aside, and help others get ahead. Don't be obsessed with getting your own advantage. Forget yourselves long enough to lend a helping hand.

Philippians 2:1–4 MSG

· Church ·

For me (Rachel), especially as a pastor's wife, I've sometimes found church to be a lonely place. Sunday mornings I get our daughters ready for church by myself, walk in with the girls by myself, sit by myself, and leave with the girls by myself. Of course, I talk with people and engage when I'm there, but it often feels as if no one really knows me.

Pastor's wife or not, I know I'm not alone in feeling like the church can be a lonely place. The main thing that has helped with this feeling of aloneness is spending time with the church community *outside* of the church building. The more time I spend with our church community group, or other moms who go to our church, the less alone I feel, the less it's about me, and the more I'm able to receive the community that God has given me to help me grow and know Jesus.

Tim Keller wrote, "It is not enough to simply show up at a church service where you live physically, but then try to maintain all your closest relationships with friends and family members who live far away. . . . [I]f we are going to give and receive grace from each other, we have to get it the way God gave it to us. We have to be involved in accountable friendships and deep relationships with other people where we live."[1]

God asks believers to gather together.

 Hebrews 10:24–25 Let us think of ways to motivate one another to acts of love and good works. And let us not neglect our meeting

together, as some people do, but encourage one another, especially now that the day of his return is drawing near. (NLT)

Christian theology tells us we were made in the image of God, and that God is a Trinity. Jesus said he never did anything, said anything, or accomplished anything without his Father. The persons of the Trinity are absolutely one—each person does everything with the others. We were meant to live like that.[2]

Tim Keller

Christ loves the church as a husband loves his wife.

Ephesians 5:25–27 Husbands, love your wives, as Christ loved the church and gave himself up for her, that he might sanctify her, having cleansed her by the washing of water with the word, so that he might present the church to himself in splendor, without spot or wrinkle or any such thing, that she might be holy and without blemish. (ESV)

The hope of the world is not government, academia, business, but the church because it is to the church that God has entrusted the message of salvation, which truly changes people's lives and hearts.[3]

Matt Perman

Community is a vital aspect of living well and as God intended.

John 13:34–35 So now I am giving you a new commandment: Love each other. Just as I have loved you, you should love each other. Your love for one another will prove to the world that you are my disciples. (NLT)

Galatians 6:2 Bear one another's burdens, and so fulfill the law of Christ. (ESV)

Romans 15:7 Therefore, accept each other just as Christ has accepted you so that God will be given glory. (NLT)

Ephesians 4:2 Be patient with each other, making allowance for each other's faults because of your love. (NLT)

The church, at its core, is about people who were dead in their sins and who are now alive through Christ.

1 Corinthians 6:9–11 Or do you not know that wrongdoers will not inherit the kingdom of God? Do not be deceived: Neither the sexually immoral nor idolaters nor adulterers nor men who have sex with men nor thieves nor the greedy nor drunkards nor slanderers nor swindlers will inherit the kingdom of God. And that is what some of you were. But you were washed, you were sanctified, you were justified in the name of the Lord Jesus Christ and by the Spirit of our God. (NIV)

· ·

The church is a hospital for sinners, not a museum for saints.[4]

Abigail VanBuren

· ·

Believers need each other for the body of Christ to function as God planned.

Romans 12:4–5 Just as our bodies have many parts and each part has a special function, so it is with Christ's body. We are many parts of one body, and we all belong to each other. (NLT)

1 Corinthians 12:26 If one member suffers, all suffer together; if one member is honored, all rejoice together. (ESV)

Church leaders are to be honored and respected.

1 Thessalonians 5:12–13 Dear brothers and sisters, honor those who are your leaders in the Lord's work. They work hard among you and give you spiritual guidance. Show them great respect and wholehearted love because of their work. And live peacefully with each other. (NLT)

Submission to the leadership of church authorities is God's will, as long as they are submissive to God's Word.

Hebrews 13:17 Obey your leaders and submit to them, for they are keeping watch over your souls, as those who will have to give an account. Let them do this with joy and not with groaning, for that would be of no advantage to you. (ESV)

PRACTICAL LIVING

- Read Tim Keller's essay "The Difficulty of Community" (available online at TimothyKeller.com/blog).
- If you are not actively attending church, the first step is to find a church home. Learn about a few churches in your area, study what these churches believe, and pick one that actively loves Jesus and their community, and preaches the gospel.
- Make it a central priority to be fully involved in your church community with your time, finances, service, and affection.
- Serve within your church community. This is the difference between being just a consumer and being someone who is invested in the health and growth of your community.

- Know and be known: join a church small group or Bible study. Allow trusted people within these communities to truly know you. Share your life and join in the lives of others.
- See related topics: Hospitality, Forgiving Others, and the Knowing God section.

RECOMMENDED READING

- *Why We Love the Church*. Kevin DeYoung and Ted Cluck. Moody.
- *Culture Shock*. Chip Ingram. Baker.
- *Spirituality for the Rest of Us*. Larry Osborne. Multnomah.
- *Life Together*. Dietrich Bonhoeffer. HarperOne.
- *Bread and Wine*. Shauna Niequist. Zondervan.

· Communication ·

A bit in the mouth of a horse controls the whole horse. A small rudder on a huge ship in the hands of a skilled captain sets a course in the face of the strongest winds. A word out of your mouth may seem of no account, but it can accomplish nearly anything—or destroy it!

James 3:3–5 MSG

. . . .

Every word we speak must be up to God's standard and according to his design.[1]

Paul Tripp

. . . .

Positive qualities to develop in speech:

Encouraging

 Ephesians 4:29 Let no corrupting talk come out of your mouths, but only such as is good for building up, as fits the occasion, that it may give grace to those who hear. (ESV)

Gentle

Proverbs 15:1 A gentle answer turns away wrath, but a harsh word stirs up anger. (NASB)

Patient

Proverbs 25:15 With patience a ruler may be persuaded, and a soft tongue will break a bone. (ESV)

Truthful

Ephesians 4:25 Therefore, having put away falsehood, let each one of you speak the truth with his neighbor, for we are members one of another. (ESV)

Thoughtful

Proverbs 18:13 If one gives an answer before he hears, it is his folly and shame. (ESV)

Proverbs 15:28 The heart of the godly thinks carefully before speaking; the mouth of the wicked overflows with evil words. (NLT)

Knowledgeable

Proverbs 20:15 There is gold, and an abundance of jewels; but the lips of knowledge are a more precious thing. (NASB)

Appropriate

Proverbs 10:19 Too much talk leads to sin. Be sensible and keep your mouth shut. (NLT)

Proverbs 25:11 A word fitly spoken is like apples of gold in a setting of silver. (ESV)

Kind

Proverbs 16:24 Kind words are like honey—sweet to the soul and healthy for the body. (NLT)

Proverbs 12:25 Worry can rob you of happiness, but kind words will cheer you up. (GNT)

Proverbs 18:21 Words kill, words give life; they're either poison or fruit—you choose. (MSG)

Negative qualities to avoid in speech:

Misusing God's name

Exodus 20:7 You shall not misuse the name of the LORD your God, for the LORD will not hold anyone guiltless who misuses his name. (NIV)

Unwholesome

Ephesians 4:29–30 Do not let any unwholesome talk come out of your mouths, but only what is helpful for building others up according to their needs, that it may benefit those who listen. And do not grieve the Holy Spirit of God, with whom you were sealed for the day of redemption. (NIV)

James 3:7–12

This is scary: You can tame a tiger, but you can't tame a tongue—it's never been done. The tongue runs wild, a wanton killer. With our tongues we bless God our Father; with the same tongues we curse the very men and women he made in his image. Curses and blessings out of the same mouth! My friends, this can't go on. A spring doesn't gush fresh water one day and brackish the next, does it? . . . You're not going to dip into a polluted mud hole and get a cup of clear, cool water, are you? (MSG)

Crude

Ephesians 5:4 Let there be no filthiness nor foolish talk nor crude joking, which are out of place, but instead let there be thanksgiving. (ESV)

Deceitful

Colossians 3:9–10 Do not lie to one another, seeing that you have put off the old self with its practices and have put on the new self, which is being renewed in knowledge after the image of its creator. (ESV)

Too quick to speak

Proverbs 18:17 The first one to plead his cause seems right, until his neighbor comes and examines him. (NKJV)

Foolish and ignorant

2 Timothy 2:23–24 But keep away from foolish and ignorant arguments; you know that they end up in quarrels. As the Lord's

James 3:5–6

It only takes a spark, remember, to set off a forest fire. A careless or wrongly placed word out of your mouth can do that. By our speech we can ruin the world, turn harmony to chaos, throw mud on a reputation, send the whole world up in smoke and go up in smoke with it, smoke right from the pit of hell. (MSG)

servant, you must not quarrel. You must be kind toward all, a good and patient teacher. (GNT)

Gossip

Proverbs 20:19 A gossip goes around telling secrets, so don't hang around with chatterers. (NLT)

Ephesians 4:31 Let all bitterness and wrath and anger and clamor and slander be put away from you, along with all malice. (ESV)

Lack of control

James 1:26 If you claim to be religious but don't control your tongue, you are fooling yourself, and your religion is worthless. (NLT)

Complaining

Philippians 2:14 Do everything without complaining or arguing. (GNT)

Lying

Ephesians 4:25 Therefore, putting away lying, "Let each one of you speak truth with his neighbor," for we are members of one another. (NKJV)

1 John 2:21 I have not written to you because you do not know the truth, but because you know it, and that no lie is of the truth. (NKJV)

When we are not honest with each other, we actually do Satan's work for him, acting as his agents, deceiving and destroying each other.[2]

Nancy DeMoss

PRACTICAL LIVING

- Choose a few of the Scriptures above, write them on 3x5 cards, and place them around your home as reminders.
- Be intentional: every day choose at least one person to encourage with your words.
- Pray for healthy speech patterns. Pray that God will help you to control your tongue and use it to build up others, rather than tear them down.
- Evaluate speech habits from your childhood and current home life. List godly and negative speech patterns.
- Practice not using speech to accuse others.
- Journal past speech errors and sins. How could applying Scripture have changed those situations? Ask for forgiveness and move on.

- Pray before you go into social situations, before calling or writing someone, or posting on a social media site.
- Consider those situations where you lied. Evaluate the reasons—was it fear of others? Fear of being exposed? Of losing friends? Rejection? Pride? Recognize your need to see lying as God sees it.

RECOMMENDED READING

- *War of Words*. Paul David Tripp. P&R.
- *Reclaiming Conversation: The Power of Talk in a Digital Age*. Sherry Turkle. Penguin.
- *The Peacemaker*. Ken Sande. Baker.
- *Pursuit of Holiness*. Jerry Bridges. NavPress.
- *Respectable Sins: Confronting the Sins We Tolerate*. Jerry Bridges. NavPress.
- *Lies Women Believe and the Truth That Sets Them Free*. Nancy Leigh DeMoss. Moody.

· Forgiving Others ·

Read the topic "Sin and God's Forgiveness." The first step to truly forgiving others is recognizing how much you've been forgiven.

True forgiveness is costly. It does not mean, "It's okay that you hurt me." It does not mean, "It wasn't a big deal." Forgiveness is not excusing a wrong. True forgiveness means, "I will take this burden. I will forgive the inexcusable. What you did is *not okay*, it is a *big deal*. But I forgive because God has forgiven the inexcusable in me." There's always a cost to forgiveness. Someone pays a price. We forgive others because Jesus paid the ultimate cost when he forgave our inexcusable sin on the cross.

Ken Sande explains what forgiveness is and isn't: "Forgiveness is not a feeling. Forgiveness is not forgetting. Forgiveness is not excusing. Forgiveness is a decision. As someone once said, 'Unforgiveness is the poison we drink, hoping others with die.' Your other choice is to make payments on the debt and thereby release others from penalties they deserve to pay."[1]

. . . .

To be a Christian means to forgive the inexcusable, because God has forgiven the inexcusable in you.[2]

C. S. Lewis

. . . .

Forgiving others is not an option; it is a step of obedience.

Colossians 3:13–14 Bear with each other and forgive one another if any of you has a grievance against someone. Forgive as the Lord forgave you. And over all these virtues put on love, which binds them all together in perfect unity. (NIV)

 Ephesians 4:32 Be kind and compassionate to one another, forgiving each other, just as in Christ God forgave you. (NIV)

Matthew 6:14–15 If you forgive those who sin against you, your heavenly Father will forgive you. But if you refuse to forgive others, your Father will not forgive your sins. (NLT)

Forgiveness is an act of the will, and the will can function regardless of the temperature of the heart.[3]

Corrie Ten Boom and Jamie Buckingham

Do not keep a record of how many times you forgive.

Matthew 18:21–22 Then Peter came up and said to him, "Lord, how often will my brother sin against me, and I forgive him? As many as seven times?" Jesus said to him, "I do not say to you seven times, but seventy seven times." (ESV)

PRACTICAL LIVING

- Journal your thoughts as you read Matthew 18:21–35. How does this Scripture change how you forgive others? What would it be like if God did not forgive us? Does that change your heart for forgiving others?

- Write these statements on cards and post them: 1) Forgiveness is not a feeling but an action. 2) Forgiveness is a choice of obedience to God. 3) Forgiveness does not mean the other person was right. 4) Forgiveness offers freedom.

- Every time you remember a past wrong, make sure you no longer hold it to the offender's account. It is forgiven.

- Read Genesis 50. How was Joseph wronged? What was his response?

RECOMMENDED READING

. . . .

- *Free of Charge.* Miroslav Volf. Zondervan.
- *Unpacking Forgiveness.* Chris Brauns. Crossway.
- *From Forgiving to Forgiven.* Jay Adams. Calvary Press.
- *Freedom from Resentment* (booklet). Robert Jones. CCEF.
- *The Peacemaker.* Ken Sande. Baker.

· Friendship ·

True friendship is a sacred, important thing, and it happens when we drop down into that deeper level of who we are, when we cross over into the broken, fragile parts of ourselves. We have to give something up in order to get friendship like that. We have to give up our need to be perceived as perfect. We have to give up our ability to control what people think of us. We have to overcome the fear that when they see the depths of who we are, they'll leave. But what we give up is nothing in comparison to what this kind of friendship gives us. Friendship is about risk. Love is about risk. If we can control it and manage it and manufacture it, then it's something else, but if it's really love, really friendship, it's a little scary around the edges.[1]

Shauna Niequist

It is important to establish and maintain friendships that honor God.

Proverbs 12:26 The righteous should choose his friends carefully, for the way of the wicked leads them astray. (NKJV)

Choose friends wisely; choose godly influences.

Proverbs 13:20 Walk with the wise and become wise; associate with fools and get in trouble. (NLT)

Ecclesiastes 4:10 If one person falls, the other can reach out and help. But someone who falls alone is in real trouble. (NLT)

1 Thessalonians 5:11 Therefore encourage one another and build up one another, just as you also are doing. (NASB)

Loyalty is a mark of a good friend. What kind of a friend are you?

Ecclesiastes 4:12 A person standing alone can be attacked and defeated, but two can stand back-to-back and conquer. Three are even better, for a triple-braided cord is not easily broken. (NLT)

Romans 15:7 Accept one another, then, just as Christ accepted you, in order to bring praise to God. (NIV)

Galatians 6:2 Bear one another's burdens, and thereby fulfill the law of Christ. (NASB)

At times, earthly friends will fail us.

Psalm 55:12–14 It is not an enemy who taunts me—I could bear that. It is not my foes who so arrogantly insult me—I could have hidden from them. Instead, it is you—my equal, my companion and close friend. What good fellowship we once enjoyed as we walked together to the house of God. (NLT)

Psalm 41:9 Even my close friend in whom I trusted, who ate my bread, has lifted his heel against me. (ESV)

. . . .

The disappointments of relationships are many, but his grace is sufficient—in fact, it is made perfect in your weakness.[2]

Paul Tripp

. . . .

Our heavenly Father will never fail us.

Joshua 1:9 Have I not commanded you? Be strong and courageous. Do not be frightened, and do not be dismayed, for the LORD your God is with you wherever you go. (ESV)

Joshua 21:45 Not one of the good promises which the LORD had made to the house of Israel failed; all came to pass. (NASB)

Friendships should not be made merely for personal advancement or gain.

Proverbs 19:4–7 Wealth makes many "friends"; poverty drives them all away. A false witness will not go unpunished, nor will a liar escape. Many seek favors from a ruler; everyone is the friend of a person who gives gifts! The relatives of the poor despise them; how much more will their friends avoid them! Though the poor plead with them, their friends are gone. (NLT)

Romans 12:10 Be devoted to one another in love. Honor one another above yourselves. (NIV)

When possible, restore broken friendships.

Romans 12:18 Do all that you can to live in peace with everyone. (NLT)

Proverbs 19:11 Good sense makes one slow to anger, and it is his glory to overlook an offense. (ESV)

Ephesians 4:32 Be kind to one another, tenderhearted, forgiving one another, as God in Christ forgave you. (ESV)

Ephesians 4:3 Make every effort to keep the unity of the Spirit through the bond of peace. (NIV)

When choosing friends or a spouse, avoid those with anger issues.

Proverbs 22:24–25 Don't hang out with angry people; don't keep company with hotheads. Bad temper is contagious—don't get infected. (MSG)

Proverbs 21:9 It's better to live alone in the corner of an attic than with a quarrelsome wife in a lovely home. (NLT)

. . . .

[Friendship] is born at the moment when one man says to another "What! You too? I thought that no one but myself . . ."[3]

C. S. Lewis

. . . .

PRACTICAL LIVING

- Think through and write a list of qualities you look for in friends. Are these qualities in your own life?
- It's dangerous when the best things in our lives become ultimate things. Evaluate your choices and friendships as you read the book *Counterfeit Gods* by Tim Keller.
- Pray for opportunities to be a good friend.

- Friendships should be life-giving. Sadly, they can also be toxic—read the essay "When Is It Time to Walk Away?" by Jen Hatmaker (available online at JenHatmaker.com/blog).
- Read the book of Ruth. What are some ways that Ruth was a steadfast friend to Naomi?
- Write encouraging notes to your friends.
- Take the initiative to befriend someone. Invite her to do something with you, or offer to serve her in some way.
- See related topics: Communication, Loneliness, Hospitality, Church, and Forgiving Others.

RECOMMENDED READING

- *Getting to the Heart of Friendships*. Amy Baker. Focus.
- *Cold Tangerines*. Shauna Niequist. Zondervan.
- *Bread and Wine*. Shauna Niequist. Zondervan.
- *Relationships: A Mess Worth Making*. Paul David Tripp and Tim Lane. David C. Cook.
- *The Peacemaker*. Ken Sande. Baker Publishing.
- *Picking Up the Pieces: Recovering Broken Relationships*. Lou Priolo. P&R.
- *Messy Beautiful Friendship*. Christine Hoover. Baker.
- *For the Love*. Jen Hatmaker. Thomas Nelson.

· Hospitality ·

The word *hospitality* in the New Testament translates literally "love of strangers." We cannot love God unless we love each other, and to love we must know each other. We know Him in the breaking of bread, and we know each other in the breaking of bread, and we are not alone anymore. Heaven is a banquet and life is a banquet, too, even with a crust, where there is companionship.[1]

Dorothy Day

Hospitality is commanded.

 Romans 12:13 When God's people are in need, be ready to help them. Always be eager to practice hospitality. (NLT)

1 Peter 4:9 Show hospitality to one another without grumbling. (ESV)

Hebrews 13:1–2 Let brotherly love continue. Do not neglect to show hospitality to strangers, for thereby some have entertained angels unawares. (ESV)

Use hospitality to cross social barriers.

Luke 14:12–14 Then [Jesus] turned to the host. "The next time you put on a dinner, don't just invite your friends and family and rich neighbors, the kind of people who will return the favor. Invite some people who never get invited out, the misfits from the wrong side of the tracks. You'll be—and experience—a blessing. They won't be able to return the favor, but the favor will be returned—oh, how it will be returned!—at the resurrection of God's people." (MSG)

Romans 12:20–21 Our Scriptures tell us that if you see your enemy hungry, go buy that person lunch, or if he's thirsty, get him a drink. Your generosity will surprise him with goodness. Don't let evil get the best of you; get the best of evil by doing good. (MSG)

When you offer peace instead of division, when you offer faith instead of fear, when you offer someone a place at your table instead of keeping them out because they're different or messy or wrong somehow, you represent the heart of Christ.[2]

Shauna Niequist

Hospitality is a joy and a gift.

Proverbs 11:25 The generous will prosper; those who refresh others will themselves be refreshed. (NLT)

Proverbs 22:9 He who is generous will be blessed, for he gives some of his food to the poor. (NASB)

Acts 2:46–47 They worshiped together at the Temple each day, met in homes for the Lord's Supper, and shared their meals with great joy and generosity—all the while praising God and enjoying the goodwill of all the people. And each day the Lord added to their fellowship those who were being saved. (NLT)

A meal engages personal participation at the most basic level of our lives. It is virtually impossible to be detached and uninvolved when we are sharing a meal with someone.[3]

Eugene Peterson

Hospitality is an outpouring of love.

Acts 16:15 After she was baptized, along with everyone in her household, she said in a surge of hospitality, "If you're confident that I'm in this with you and believe in the Master truly, come home with me and be my guests." We hesitated, but she wouldn't take no for an answer. (MSG)

Acts 16:32–34 The jailer made them feel at home, dressed their wounds, and then—he couldn't wait till morning!—was baptized, he and everyone in his family. There in his home, he had food set out for a festive meal. It was a night to remember: He and his entire family had put their trust in God; everyone in the house was in on the celebration. (MSG)

The heart of hospitality is about creating space for someone to feel seen and heard and loved. It's about declaring your table a safe zone, a place of warmth and nourishment.[4]

Shauna Niequist

Hospitality is among the qualifications for a good leader.

1 Timothy 3:2 Therefore an overseer must be above reproach, the husband of one wife, sober-minded, self-controlled, respectable, hospitable, able to teach. (ESV)

I'm not talking about cooking as performance, or entertaining as a complicated choreography of competition and showing off. I'm talking about feeding someone with honesty and intimacy and love, about making your home a place where people are fiercely protected, even if just for a few hours, from the crush and cruelty of the day.[5]

Shauna Niequist

. . . .

PRACTICAL LIVING

. . . .

- Make a list of reasons why providing hospitality is a challenge for you. Look for fear, perfectionism, pride, selfishness, etc. Compare your reasons with scriptural commands.
- Set a goal for inviting people into your home. Start small, with something attainable. Could you have someone over for dinner once a week? Once a month? Every other month? The important thing is to start.
- Read Sarah's story, "How One Woman Created a Community Out of a Neighborhood" (available online at StorylineBlog.com). Even if it's on a much smaller scale, how can you follow her example?
- Watch the movies *The Hundred-Foot Journey* and *Babette's Feast*.
- Start a supper club. Read the chapter "Supper Club" in Jen Hatmaker's book *For the Love*.
- Practice having people in your home who may not always be invited out (a single mom and children, a widow, college-age people, those away from home).
- Bake items or take meals to those who have needs. Enclose a personal note.
- Show hospitality to a variety of age groups, backgrounds, and faiths.
- Make your home a place of peace, refuge, and rest.
- See related topics: Church and Friendship.

RECOMMENDED READING

- *Bread and Wine: A Love Letter to Life Around the Table with Recipes*. Shauna Niequist. Zondervan.
- *Practicing Hospitality*. Pat Ennis. Crossway.
- *Untamed Hospitality*. Elizabeth Newman. Brazos.
- *The Reluctant Entertainer*. Sandy Coughlin. Bethany House.
- *For the Love*. Jen Hatmaker. Thomas Nelson.
- *The Nesting Place*. Myquillyn Smith. Harper Collins.

· Marriage ·

Marriage is not ultimately about sex or social stability or personal fulfillment; rather, marriage was created to be a human reflection of the ultimate love relationship with the Lord. . . . It points to the true marriage that our souls need and the true family our hearts want. No marriage can ultimately give us what we most desire and truly need. . . . [E]ven Christians married to Christians will do a terrible job of conducting their marriage if they lack a love relationship with Christ.[1]

Tim Keller

God created marriage. It's a covenant—sacred and meant to last.

Genesis 2:18, 22–25 Then the LORD God said, "It is not good for the man to be alone; I will make him a helper suitable for him."

... The LORD God fashioned into a woman the rib which He had taken from the man, and brought her to the man. The man said, "This is now bone of my bones, and flesh of my flesh; she shall be called Woman, because she was taken out of Man." For this reason a man shall leave his father and his mother, and be joined to his wife; and they shall become one flesh. And the man and his wife were both naked and were not ashamed. (NASB)

 Matthew 19:6 So they are no longer two, but one flesh. What therefore God has joined together, let no man separate. (NASB)

The love of a husband and wife is compared to Christ's own love for the church.

Ephesians 5:25–27 Husbands, love your wives, just as Christ loved the church and gave himself up for her to make her holy, cleansing her by the washing with water through the word, and to present her to himself as a radiant church, without stain or wrinkle or any other blemish, but holy and blameless. (NIV)

Marriage is honorable.

Hebrews 13:4 Marriage is to be held in honor among all, and the marriage bed is to be undefiled; for fornicators and adulterers God will judge. (NASB)

Proverbs 18:22 He who finds a wife finds a good thing and obtains favor from the LORD. (NASB)

Marriage is meant to be a signpost of God's love and commitment to us.

James 1:17 Every good and perfect gift is from above, coming down from the Father of the heavenly lights, who does not change like shifting shadows. (NIV)

Ephesians 5:31–32 "For this reason a man will leave his father and mother and be united to his wife, and the two will become one flesh." This is a profound mystery—but I am talking about Christ and the church. (NIV)

. . . .

One of the main purposes of marriage is . . . to show the world how Christ transforms everything, including marriage.[2]

Tim Keller

. . . .

Marriage is a good thing, but not an ultimate thing.

Psalm 62:5–8 For God alone, O my soul, wait in silence, for my hope is from him. He only is my rock and my salvation, my fortress; I shall not be shaken. On God rests my salvation and my glory; my mighty rock, my refuge is God. Trust in him at all times, O people; pour out your heart before him; God is a refuge for us. (ESV)

Matthew 22:29 But Jesus answered them, "You are wrong, because you know neither the Scriptures nor the power of God. For in the resurrection they neither marry nor are given in marriage, but are like angels in heaven." (ESV)

Deuteronomy 6:5 Love the LORD your God with all your heart and with all your soul and with all your strength. (NIV)

Marriage can be lonely. God can redeem broken situations. Nothing is impossible.

Jeremiah 32:17 Ah, Lord GOD! It is you who have made the heavens and the earth by your great power and by your outstretched arm! Nothing is too hard for you. (ESV)

Matthew 19:26 Jesus looked at them intently and said, "Humanly speaking, it is impossible. But with God everything is possible." (NLT)

Lamentations 3:21–23 This I recall to mind, therefore I have hope. The LORD's lovingkindnesses indeed never cease, for His compassions never fail. They are new every morning; great is Your faithfulness. (NASB)

Husbands are uniquely called to Christlike self-sacrifice.

Ephesians 5:25–33 Husbands, go all out in your love for your wives, exactly as Christ did for the church—a love marked by giving, not getting. Christ's love makes the church whole. His words evoke her beauty. Everything he does and says is designed to bring the best out of her, dressing her in dazzling white silk, radiant with holiness. And that is how husbands ought to love their wives. They're really doing themselves a favor—since they're already "one" in marriage. No one abuses his own body, does he? No, he feeds and pampers it. That's how Christ treats us, the church, since we are part of his body. And this is why a man leaves father and mother and cherishes his wife. No longer two, they become "one flesh." This is a huge mystery, and I don't pretend to understand it all. What is clearest to me is the way Christ treats the church. And this provides a good picture of how each husband is to treat his wife, loving himself in loving her, and how each wife is to honor her husband. (MSG)

Wives are uniquely called to Christlike submission.

Ephesians 5:22–24 Wives, understand and support your husbands in ways that show your support for Christ. The husband provides leadership to his wife the way Christ does to his church, not by domineering but by cherishing. So just as the church submits to Christ as he exercises such leadership, wives should likewise submit to their husbands. (MSG)

This is where Jesus comes in. . . . It takes both men and women, living out their gender roles in the safety of home and church, to reveal to the world the fullness of the person of Jesus.[3]

Kathy Keller

Submission to God, and his Word, is the first priority.

Acts 5:29 Peter and the other apostles replied: "We must obey God rather than human beings!" (NIV)

Believers should only marry other believers.

2 Corinthians 6:14 Do not be bound together with unbelievers; for what partnership have righteousness and lawlessness, or what fellowship has light with darkness? (NASB)

Marriage is a permanent commitment.

Mark 10:7–9 "For this reason a man will leave his father and mother and be united to his wife, and the two will become one flesh." So they are no longer two, but one flesh. Therefore what God has joined together, let no one separate. (NIV)

PRACTICAL LIVING

- Together with your spouse or fiancé, listen to Tim Keller's series "Sex, Singleness, and Marriage" (available online at GospelInLife.com).
- Listen to the sermon "Sexuality and Christian Hope" by Tim Keller (available online at GospelInLife.com).
- Pray *with* your spouse on a regular basis.

- You and your spouse can each make a list of seven things that are life-giving and bring you joy (for example, one of mine [Rachel] is "quality and restful family time"). Then, each of you can make a list of seven things in your life that are soul-crushing (for example, "when I'm not truly heard or understood"). These lists could be about marriage, work, occupations, friendships, family, hobbies, etc. Finally, plan a time where you and your spouse can discuss your lists together.
- Pray for your spouse on a regular basis.
- As a couple, write out goals for how you want your marriage to honor God.
- Schedule regular date nights.
- Marriage can often be a place of loneliness, misunderstanding, and heartbreak. Don't hesitate to seek counseling, whether individually or as a couple, depending on the situation.
- Read the essay on mutual submission entitled "Women, Stop Submitting to Men" by Russell Moore (available online at RussellMoore.com).
- See related topics: Marital Sex, Hope, Divorce, Adultery, and Forgiving Others.

RECOMMENDED READING

- *The Meaning of Marriage.* Tim and Kathy Keller. Penguin.
- *Jesus, Justice, and Gender Roles.* Kathy Keller. Zondervan.
- *What Did You Expect? Redeeming the Realities of Marriage.* Paul Tripp. Crossway.
- *When Sinners Say "I Do."* Dave Harvey. Shepherd.

· Mothering ·

I shared with my mom when my oldest son was a few months old that mothering was the most self-sacrificing thing I have ever done. Now, as I look at my eighteen-year-old son, I am reminded that I love being a mother. He still likes to be around me, looks for my advice, and is sensitive to the things of the Lord. He loves God and people and he still wants to sit on my lap, although I can only take it for about thirty seconds since he is so big! How did this happen—this end of childhood, this spiritual maturity? God did it, and he chose to use me. He chose to use me through a thousand little ordinary moments surrendered to him through pain, sacrifice, and lots of joy. Mothering is the gospel lived out as you hold your child's heart in beauty, prayer, and patience. It's not the big decisions, but the little ones, trusting God through it all.[1]

Elizabeth Hawn

Our identities are found in Christ, not in our role as mothers.

Philippians 3:8–9 Yes, everything else is worthless when compared with the infinite value of knowing Christ Jesus my Lord. For his sake I have discarded everything else, counting it all as garbage, so that I could gain Christ and become one with him. I no longer count on my own righteousness through obeying the law; rather, I become righteous through faith in Christ. For God's way of making us right with himself depends on faith. (NLT)

The Christian mom doesn't love Jesus instead of loving her children; she loves Jesus by loving her children.[2]

Jen Wilkin

Our significance is based on our relationship with God, not on any personal qualities or the achievements of our children.

> Ephesians 2:10 For we are his workmanship, created in Christ Jesus for good works, which God prepared beforehand, that we should walk in them. (ESV)

> 2 Corinthians 5:17 Therefore, if anyone is in Christ, he is a new creation. The old has passed away; behold, the new has come. (ESV)

> Micah 6:8 He has shown you, O mortal, what is good. And what does the LORD require of you? To act justly and to love mercy and to walk humbly with your God. (NIV)

. . . .

A mom whose love of her kids is motivated by their achievements or behavior has identity issues. If she has to raise the perfect child in order to feel at peace about her worth, her identity is misplaced. By asking motherhood to be her savior, she reveals not that she loves her kids too much, but too little.[3]

Jen Wilkin

. . . .

Children are a gift and blessing from the Lord.

> Psalm 127:3–5 Don't you see that children are GOD's best gift? The fruit of the womb his generous legacy? Like a warrior's fistful of arrows are the children of a vigorous youth. Oh, how blessed are you parents, with your quivers full of children! Your enemies don't stand a chance against you; you'll sweep them right off your doorstep. (MSG)

Teaching our children about God is a vital part of mothering.

Deuteronomy 6:4–9 Listen, O Israel! The LORD is our God, the LORD alone. And you must love the LORD your God with all your heart, all your soul, and all your strength. And you must commit yourselves wholeheartedly to these commands that I am giving you today. Repeat them again and again to your children. Talk about them when you are at home and when you are on the road, when you are going to bed and when you are getting up. Tie them to your hands and wear them on your forehead as reminders. Write them on the doorposts of your house and on your gates. (NLT)

Tender parenting is a frequent theme of Scripture.

Isaiah 40:11 He will feed His flock like a shepherd; He will gather the lambs with His arm, and carry them in His bosom, and gently lead those who are with young. (NKJV)

Isaiah 49:15 Can a woman forget her nursing child, and not have compassion on the son of her womb? Surely they may forget, yet I will not forget you. (NKJV)

Isaiah 66:13 As one whom his mother comforts, so I will comfort you; and you shall be comforted in Jerusalem. (NKJV)

1 Thessalonians 2:7 But we were gentle among you, just as a nursing mother cherishes her own children. (NKJV)

. . . .

Jesus taught that providing shelter for the shelterless, food for the hungry, and clothing for the naked are sacred acts. They're also the hallmark activities of mothering. When we do them from the right motive for those in our homes, it's as if we've done them for Christ himself (Matt. 25:31–45).[4]

Jen Wilkin

. . . .

Treat your children like you would your neighbor—people created and loved by God.[5]

Mark 12:30–31 "Love the Lord your God with all your heart and with all your soul and with all your mind and with all your strength." The second is this: "Love your neighbor as yourself." There is no commandment greater than these. (NIV)

Ephesians 4:2 Always be humble and gentle. Be patient with each other, making allowance for each other's faults because of your love. (NLT)

Ephesians 4:29–32 Let no unwholesome word proceed from your mouth, but only such a word as is good for edification according to the need of the moment, so that it will give grace to those who hear. . . . Let all bitterness and wrath and anger and clamor and slander be put away from you, along with all malice. Be kind to one another, tender-hearted, forgiving each other, just as God in Christ also has forgiven you. (NASB)

1 Peter 3:8–9 Finally, all of you, have unity of mind, sympathy, brotherly love, a tender heart, and a humble mind. Do not repay evil for evil or reviling for reviling, but on the contrary, bless, for to this you were called, that you may obtain a blessing. (ESV)

. . . .

[E]very scriptural imperative that speaks to loving our neighbor as we love ourselves suddenly comes to bear on how we parent. Every command to love preferentially at great cost, with great effort, and with godly wisdom becomes not just a command to love the people in my workplace or the people in my church . . . or the people in the homeless shelter. It becomes a command to love the people under my own roof, no matter how small. If children are people, then our own children are our very closest neighbors. No other neighbor lives closer or needs our self-sacrificing love more.[6]

Jen Wilkin

. . . .

Discipline is an important part of mothering.

Proverbs 19:18 Discipline your children while there is hope. Otherwise you will ruin their lives. (NLT)

Proverbs 22:6 Start children off on the way they should go, and even when they are old they will not turn from it. (NIV)

God understands the pain of having children willfully disobey.

Jeremiah 3:22 "My wayward children," says the LORD, "come back to me, and I will heal your wayward hearts." (NLT)

Isaiah 1:2 Listen, O heavens! Pay attention, earth! This is what the LORD says: "The children I raised and cared for have rebelled against me." (NLT)

Jeremiah 6:16 Thus says the LORD: "Stand in the ways and see, and ask for the old paths, where the good way is, and walk in it; then you will find rest for your souls. But they said, 'We will not walk in it.'" (NKJV)

When we are lacking, God gives wisdom and strength.

James 1:2–5 Consider it all joy, my brethren, when you encounter various trials, knowing that the testing of your faith produces endurance. And let endurance have its perfect result, so that you may be perfect and complete, lacking in nothing. But if any of you lacks wisdom, let him ask of God, who gives to all generously and without reproach, and it will be given to him. (NASB)

Pray for your children.

Lamentations 2:19 Rise during the night and cry out. Pour out your hearts like water to the LORD. Lift up your hands to him in prayer, pleading for your children. (NLT)

Romans 8:26 In the same way the Spirit also helps our weakness; for we do not know how to pray as we should, but the Spirit Himself intercedes for us with groanings too deep for words. (NASB)

Matthew 7:7–11 Keep on asking, and you will receive what you ask for. Keep on seeking, and you will find. Keep on knocking, and the door will be opened to you. For everyone who asks, receives. Everyone who seeks, finds. And to everyone who knocks, the door will be opened. You parents—if your children ask for a loaf of bread, do you give them a stone instead? Or if they ask for a fish, do you give them a snake? Of course not! So if you sinful people know how to give good gifts to your children, how much more will your heavenly Father give good gifts to those who ask him. (NLT)

PRACTICAL LIVING

- Read Jen Wilkin's blog post "Our Children, Our Neighbors" (available online at JenWilkin.blogspot.com). Does seeing your child as your neighbor change how you respond to your child in difficult situations?
- Read the essay "On Empty Nests, Christian Mommy Guilt, and Misplaced Identity" by Jen Wilkin (available online at TheGospelCoalition.org). Write down how this essay changes how you parent.
- Look up these verses organized by Jen Wilkin: "Here are just a few 'unlikely' parenting verses that point me back to neighborliness on the days that don't go as they should:
  » When I want to correct my kids with harshness: *Proverbs 15:1*
  » When I want to lecture them: *James 1:19–20*
  » When I want to make them make me look awesome: *Philippians 2:3–4*

» When I find meeting their needs to be an imposition: *Matthew 25:37–40*

» When I want credit for how hard I'm working as the mom: *Matthew 6:3–4*

» When I don't want to extend forgiveness for their offenses: *Ephesians 4:31–32*

» When I've completely lost sight of the forest for the trees: *2 Timothy 2:24–26.*"[7]

• Guard your own daily time with God in his Word and prayer. The book *New Morning Mercies* by Paul David Tripp is an excellent place to start.

• Read *The Jesus Storybook Bible* by Sally Lloyd-Jones aloud as a family.

• Look for ways to make your home a place of refuge and peace.

• Listen to the online workshop with Jen Wilkin, "Raising an Alien Child" (available at TheGospelCoalition.org).

• See related topics: Self-Worth, Communication, Work, Rest, Trust, Hope, and Worry.

RECOMMENDED READING

• *Parenting: 14 Gospel Principles That Can Radically Change Your Family*. Paul David Tripp. Crossway.

• *Spiritual Parenting*. Michelle Anthony. David C. Cook.

• *Becoming a Spiritually Healthy Family*. Michelle Anthony. David C. Cook.

• *Shepherding a Child's Heart*. Ted Tripp. Shepherd Press.

• "Christian Subculture and the Stay-At-Home-Mom." Jen Wilkin. (Available online at JenWilkin.blogspot.com.)

- *The Gospel-Centered Parent.* Rose Miller, Deborah Harrell, Jack Klumpenhower. New Growth.
- *Making Home Work.* Paul Chappell. Striving Together Publications.
- *When Good Kids Make Bad Choices.* Elyse Fitzpatrick. Harvest House.
- *Prayers for Prodigals: 90 Days of Prayer for Your Child.* James Banks. Discovery House.

· Singleness ·

Jesus was the most whole, complete human being who walked on earth, and he was never married and never had children. His life demonstrates that marriage cannot be the ultimate life goal, nor is singleness less than a full life lived. The apostle Paul also holds up a life of singleness as equally good as a life of marriage (1 Corinthians 7:7).

Tim Keller underscores the role single adults have in God's kingdom: "Do you see how the gospel changes our view of marriage and singleness? Christians are to choose between marriage and singleness not for the basic contemporary motive of personal fulfillment, nor for the traditional motive of propagating family legacy. Rather, we are to marry or to remain single on the basis of which state best makes us a sign of the kingdom."[1]

Singleness can simplify life and devotion to Christ.

 1 Corinthians 7:28–35 But those who marry will face many troubles in this life, and I want to spare you this. What I mean, brothers and sisters, is that the time is short. . . . For this world in its present form is passing away. I would like you to be free from concern. An unmarried man is concerned about the Lord's affairs—how he can please the Lord. But a married man is concerned about the affairs of this world—how he can please his wife—and his interests are divided. An unmarried woman or virgin is concerned about the Lord's affairs: Her aim is to be devoted to the Lord in both body and spirit. But a married woman is concerned about the affairs of this world—how she can please her husband. I am saying this for your own good, not to restrict you, but that you may live in a right way in undivided devotion to the Lord. (NIV)

Marriage is a good thing, but not an ultimate thing.

Psalm 62:5–8 For God alone, O my soul, wait in silence, for my hope is from him. He only is my rock and my salvation, my fortress; I shall not be shaken. On God rests my salvation and my glory; my mighty rock, my refuge is God. Trust in him at all times, O people; pour out your heart before him; God is a refuge for us. (ESV)

Deuteronomy 6:5 Love the LORD your God with all your heart and with all your soul and with all your strength. (NIV)

. . . .

If singles don't have the same fulfilling love relationship with Jesus, they will put that pressure on their dream of marriage. . . . But if singles rest in and rejoice in their marriage to Christ, they will be able to handle single life without devastating loneliness. Singles must realize that the very same idolatry of marriage that is distorting their single life would (or will) distort their married life.[2]

Tim Keller

. . . .

The apostle Paul recommended singleness.

1 Corinthians 7:7 Sometimes I wish everyone were single like me—a simpler life in many ways! But celibacy is not for everyone any more than marriage is. God gives the gift of the single life to some, the gift of the married life to others. (MSG)

God gives hope for your future.

Isaiah 41:9–10 I have called you back from the ends of the earth, saying, "You are my servant." For I have chosen you and will not throw you away. Don't be afraid, for I am with you. Don't be discouraged, for I am your God. I will strengthen you and help you. I will hold you up with my victorious right hand. (NLT)

Jeremiah 29:11 "For I know the plans that I have for you," declares the Lord, "plans for welfare and not for calamity to give you a future and a hope." (NASB)

God is wholly committed to you.

Isaiah 54:5 For your husband is your Maker, whose name is the Lord of hosts; and your Redeemer is the Holy One of Israel, who is called the God of all the earth. (NASB)

Romans 8:38–39 For I am convinced that neither death, nor life, nor angels, nor principalities, nor things present, nor things to come, nor powers, nor height, nor depth, nor any other created thing, will be able to separate us from the love of God, which is in Christ Jesus our Lord. (NASB)

God offers strength for every situation.

Philippians 4:12–13 I know how to be brought low, and I know how to abound. In any and every circumstance, I have learned the secret of facing plenty and hunger, abundance and need. I can do all things through him who strengthens me. (ESV)

God offers his peace and his presence. You are not alone.

Psalm 46:10–11 "Cease striving and know that I am God; I will be exalted among the nations, I will be exalted in the earth." The LORD of hosts is with us; the God of Jacob is our stronghold. (NASB)

2 Corinthians 12:9 And He has said to me, "My grace is sufficient for you, for power is perfected in weakness." Most gladly, therefore, I will rather boast about my weaknesses, so that the power of Christ may dwell in me. (NASB)

Psalm 62:5–8 My soul, wait in silence for God only, for my hope is from Him. He only is my rock and my salvation, my stronghold; I shall not be shaken. On God my salvation and my glory rest; the rock of my strength, my refuge is in God. Trust in Him at all times, O people; pour out your heart before Him; God is a refuge for us. (NASB)

Jeremiah 31:3 The LORD appeared to him from afar, saying, "I have loved you with an everlasting love; therefore I have drawn you with lovingkindness." (NASB)

PRACTICAL LIVING

- Listen to Tim Keller's series "Sex, Singleness, and Marriage" (available online at GospelInLife.com).
- Read the essay on mutual submission entitled "Women, Stop Submitting to Men" by Russell Moore (available online at RussellMoore.com).
- Evaluate your involvement in your local church and community—Bible studies, serving your city, missions trips, teaching

and leadership opportunities, caregiving. Are you using your individual gifts and your singleness to their fullest potential?

- Read the essay "Sex and the Single Woman" by Fabienne Harford (available online at TheGospelCoalition.org).
- Listen to the online sermon by David Platt "Singleness and the Next Generation" (available online at Radical.net).
- Spend time studying God's sovereignty and love.
- See related topics: Church, Hospitality, Loneliness, Work, and Sexual Purity.

RECOMMENDED READING

- "The Gospel and Sex." Tim Keller. (Available online at Gospel InLife.com.)
- *The Meaning of Marriage* (especially the chapter "Singleness and Marriage"). Tim and Kathy Keller. Penguin.
- "Four Things God Says to Singles." Vaughan Roberts. (Available online at TheGospelCoalition.org.)
- *Fine China is for Single Women Too*. Carolyn Leutwiler. P&R.
- *Singleness Redefined*. Carolyn Leutwiler. P&R.
- *They Were Single Too: 8 Biblical Role Models*. David Hoffeditz. Kregel.

Difficult
Challenges

Abortion

Abortion Recovery

Abuse

Addiction

Adultery

Death

Death of a Child

Divorce

Eating Struggles

Illness

Rape

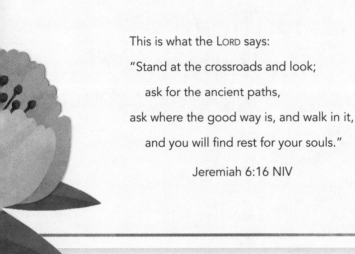

This is what the LORD says:

"Stand at the crossroads and look;

ask for the ancient paths,

ask where the good way is, and walk in it,

and you will find rest for your souls."

Jeremiah 6:16 NIV

· Abortion ·

The leading textbooks are clear: life begins at conception. That's not a religious belief. That's a scientific fact. We all started out as a microscopic zygote loaded with all the genetic information it will ever need. That's where you came from. That was you. Your life started at that moment. I don't believe life is less valuable because of its size, or its level of intelligence, or because of its relative dependence or independence, or because of where it lives. Every life is precious. Every life is a gift from God.[1]

Kevin DeYoung

Birth is not the beginning of life; it is the arrival. Note the frequent use of personal pronouns in reference to this unborn baby.

 Psalm 139:13–15 For you formed my inward parts; you knitted me together in my mother's womb. I praise you, for I am fearfully and wonderfully made. Wonderful are your works; my soul knows it very well. My frame was not hidden from you, when I was being made in secret, intricately woven in the depths of the earth. (ESV)

Isaiah 49:1 Listen to me, you islands; hear this, you distant nations: Before I was born the LORD called me; from my mother's womb he has spoken my name. (NIV)

God is actively and personally involved in the life of every unborn person, including plans for each day of his or her life.

Psalm 139:16 Your eyes saw my unformed body; all the days ordained for me were written in your book before one of them came to be. (NIV)

God has a plan for your life. God has a plan for your baby's life. Pregnancy does not take him by surprise.

Jeremiah 29:11 For I know the plans I have for you, declares the LORD, plans for welfare and not for evil, to give you a future and a hope. (ESV)

Psalm 138:8 The LORD will fulfill his purpose for me; your steadfast love, O LORD, endures forever. Do not forsake the work of your hands. (ESV)

An unborn baby is capable of joy inside the womb.

Luke 1:44 As soon as the sound of your greeting reached my ears, the baby in my womb leaped for joy. (NIV)

Our bodies are not ours—they belong to God.

Romans 12:1–2 And so, dear brothers and sisters, I plead with you to give your bodies to God because of all he has done for you. Let them be a living and holy sacrifice—the kind he will find acceptable. This is truly the way to worship him. Don't copy the behavior and customs of this world, but let God transform you into a new person by changing the way you think. Then you will learn to know God's will for you, which is good and pleasing and perfect. (NLT)

1 Corinthians 6:19–20 Don't you realize that your body is the temple of the Holy Spirit, who lives in you and was given to you

by God? You do not belong to yourself, for God bought you with a high price. So you must honor God with your body. (NLT)

Following what you desire, rather than God's plan, leads to heartache and problems.

Psalm 19:13 Keep your servant from deliberate sins! Don't let them control me. Then I will be free of guilt and innocent of great sin. (NLT)

Proverbs 14:12 There is a way that seems right to a man, but its end is the way to death. (ESV)

Proverbs 16:2 People may be pure in their own eyes, but the LORD examines their motives. (NLT)

. . . .

The child in the womb is a human being, and, from very early in the pregnancy, he or she has fingernails, a beating heart, and the capacity to feel pain. We do not become human persons by traveling a few inches down the birth canal. Every innocent life deserves a chance to live.[2]

Kevin DeYoung

. . . .

Our actions are not hidden from God.

Hebrews 4:13 Nothing in all creation is hidden from God's sight. Everything is uncovered and laid bare before the eyes of him to whom we must give account. (NIV)

Children are a gift from God, no matter the circumstances of their conception.

> Psalm 127:3–4 Behold, children are a gift of the LORD, the fruit of the womb is a reward. Like arrows in the hand of a warrior, so are the children of one's youth. (NASB)

You may desire to get out of a pregnancy and its consequences, but that is not what God desires. Choosing God's way, no matter how difficult, leads to life and peace.

> Philippians 1:9–10 And this is my prayer: that your love may abound more and more in knowledge and depth of insight, so that you may be able to discern what is best and may be pure and blameless for the day of Christ. (NIV)

> Joshua 24:14–15 Now fear the LORD and serve him with all faithfulness. Throw away the gods your ancestors worshiped beyond the Euphrates River and in Egypt, and serve the LORD. But if serving the LORD seems undesirable to you, then choose for yourselves this day whom you will serve. . . . But as for me and my household, we will serve the LORD. (NIV)

PRACTICAL LIVING

- A must-have if you are pregnant: an ultrasound, and if possible, a 3-D ultrasound. Study your baby's development.
- Wherever you are in your decision-making progress, pray that Jesus will help you to see truth and light in the midst of your situation. Pray that he will open a path in the darkness, that he will show you a way and a solution.
- Pray Philippians 4:6–7.
- Consider adoption. If you're unable to care for your baby, there's someone else longing to care for him or her.

- Visit a faith-based pregnancy center.
- Memorize Psalm 139:13–15 and say it daily.
- Memorize Isaiah 43:1–2.

RECOMMENDED READING

- *Pro-Life Answers to Pro-Choice Arguments*. Randy Alcorn. Multnomah.
- *Abortion: A Rational Look at an Emotional Issue*. R.C. Sproul. Reformation Trust Publishing.
- "Abortion" in *Culture Shock*. Chip Ingram. Baker.

· Abortion Recovery ·

Let's never forget that Jesus is God, who came to dwell among us, to make us new and to bind up our wounds. This is the Jesus we discover in the pages of Scripture, and this is the Healer I met in the areas of my deepest shame. When anyone truly encounters Him, they are transformed. His love penetrates to the deepest levels of our brokenness, bringing hope and healing.[1]

Marian Ellis

God can take a broken spirit and produce joy.

Psalm 147:3 He heals the brokenhearted and bandages their wounds. (NLT)

Psalm 51:12–17 Restore to me the joy of your salvation, and uphold me with a willing spirit. Then I will teach transgressors your ways, and sinners will return to you. Deliver me from blood-guiltiness, O God, O God of my salvation, and my tongue will sing aloud of your righteousness. O Lord, open my lips, and my mouth will declare your praise. For you will not delight in sacrifice, or I would give it; you will not be pleased with a burnt offering. The sacrifices of God are a broken spirit; a broken and contrite heart, O God, you will not despise. (ESV)

God offers restoration and freedom.

Psalm 40:1–3 I waited patiently for the LORD; he turned to me and heard my cry. He lifted me out of the slimy pit, out of the mud and mire; he set my feet on a rock and gave me a firm place to stand. He put a new song in my mouth, a hymn of praise to our God. Many will see and fear the LORD and put their trust in him. (NIV)

John 8:32, 36 Then you will know the truth, and the truth will set you free. . . . So if the Son sets you free, you will be free indeed. (NIV)

When forgiveness is requested, it is given freely.

Psalm 32:3–5 When I refused to confess my sin, my body wasted away, and I groaned all day long. Day and night your hand of discipline was heavy on me. My strength evaporated like water in the summer heat. Finally, I confessed all my sins to you and stopped trying to hide my guilt. I said to myself, I will confess my rebellion to the LORD. And you forgave me! All my guilt is gone. (NLT)

God understands sorrow for the loss of children.

Jeremiah 31:15 Thus says the LORD: "A voice was heard in Ramah, lamentation and bitter weeping, Rachel weeping for her

children, refusing to be comforted for her children, because they
are no more." (NKJV)

Once you have repented, don't dwell on your forgiven sin.

Isaiah 43:18–19 Forget the former things; do not dwell on the
past. See, I am doing a new thing! Now it springs up; do you not
perceive it? I am making a way in the wilderness and streams in
the wasteland. (NIV)

God is the only one who can save you from your sorrow.

Psalm 18:1–6 I love you, LORD, my strength. The LORD is my rock,
my fortress and my deliverer; my God is my rock, in whom I take
refuge, my shield and the horn of my salvation, my stronghold. I
called to the LORD, who is worthy of praise, and I have been saved
from my enemies. The cords of death entangled me; the torrents of
destruction overwhelmed me. The cords of the grave coiled around
me; the snares of death confronted me. In my distress I called to
the LORD; I cried to my God for help. From his temple he heard my
voice; my cry came before him, into his ears. (NIV)

Isaiah 25:8 He will swallow up death forever; and the Lord GOD
will wipe away tears from all faces, and the reproach of his people
he will take away from all the earth, for the LORD has spoken. (ESV)

Let your secret come to light. Seek a trusted community of those who love Jesus.

James 5:16 Confess your sins to each other and pray for each
other so that you may be healed. The earnest prayer of a righteous
person has great power and produces wonderful results. (NLT)

I recently asked a friend what brought about healing from her abortion. She replied, "Healing is a process. In many ways, I am still in the process. But the journey to wholeness began when I brought the secret out of the dark and into the light. As long as I kept it a secret, Satan had grounds to accuse me and to speak accusations over me. When I brought it into the light and confessed it to trusted friends who love Jesus, then I was able to begin my journey of healing. Confession is the first step of healing."[2]

Marian Ellis

PRACTICAL LIVING

- As a reminder of God's forgiveness, purchase a special piece of jewelry (perhaps a birthstone) that can be worn in memory of the baby.
- Join a Bible study with other post-abortive women. Discuss how God meets you in your need and how he can use you now.
- Visit abortion recovery websites, such as If Not For Grace Ministries and Ramah International.
- Get involved with a crisis pregnancy center and/or the pro-life movement.
- Plant a memorial tree, or conduct a memorial service.
- Focus on God's blessings in your life. Watch for them, write them down.
- Read Mindy's story at Gratefulforgrace.com.
- Read "Healing After Abortion" by Marian Jordan Ellis (available online at RedeemedGirl.org).

RECOMMENDED READING

* *Her Choice to Heal.* Syda Masse. David C. Cook.
* *Forgiven and Set Free: A Post-Abortion Bible Study for Women.* Linda Cochrane. Baker.
* *Living in His Forgiveness.* Sandy Day. Focus.
* *When the Pain Won't Go Away: Dealing with the Effects of Abortion* (booklet). Tim Jackson. RBC Ministries.
* "How Can I Get Rid of Guilt Over my Abortion?" in *Intimate Issues.* Linda Dillow. WaterBrook.

· Abuse ·

Several years ago, I (Pat) took a pair of old eyeglasses and covered the lenses with pieces of hole-punched Scotch tape. I noticed that when I spent time with women who experienced abuse, it was as if they saw themselves through distorted lenses, seeing only through the eyes of their abuse. The taped-over glasses acted as a visual, showing them how they see their world. As they held the glasses and looked through them, many of them could visualize for the first time how distorted their perception of reality had become. These women viewed their entire lives—emotions, self-worth, and families—all through the blurry distortion of abuse.

Abuse is never acceptable, whether verbal, physical, sexual, emotional, or psychological. God hates abuse. Sadly, we live in a broken and sinful world, and abuse takes many forms and shapes.

Abuse does not define a person—our identity is who we are in Christ.

The Lord Jesus himself suffered great abuse.

Isaiah 53:5–6 But he was pierced for our transgressions; he was crushed for our iniquities; upon him was the chastisement that brought us peace, and with his wounds we are healed. All we like sheep have gone astray; we have turned—every one—to his own way; and the LORD has laid on him the iniquity of us all. (ESV)

Psalm 22:7–8, 16 Everyone who sees me mocks me. They sneer and shake their heads, saying, "Is this the one who relies on the LORD? Then let the LORD save him!" . . . My enemies surround me like a pack of dogs; an evil gang closes in on me. They have pierced my hands and feet. (NLT)

When we feel alone, God is there, and we can call on him.

Zephaniah 3:17 The LORD your God is with you, the Mighty Warrior who saves. He will take great delight in you; in his love he will no longer rebuke you, but will rejoice over you with singing. (NIV)

 Psalm 142:1–7 I cry out to the LORD; I plead for the LORD's mercy. I pour out my complaints before him and tell him all my troubles. When I am overwhelmed, you alone know the way I should turn. Wherever I go, my enemies have set traps for me. I look for someone to come and help me, but no one gives me a passing thought! No one will help me; no one cares a bit what happens to me. Then I pray to you, O LORD. I say, "You are my place of refuge. You are all I really want in life. Hear my cry, for I am very low. Rescue me from my persecutors, for they are too strong for me. Bring me out of prison so I can thank you. The godly will crowd around me, for you are good to me." (NLT)

God provides strength.

Psalm 31:4 You will pull me out of the net which they have secretly laid for me, for You are my strength. (NASB)

Psalm 61:3 For You have been a refuge for me, a tower of strength against the enemy. (NASB)

Psalm 62:7 My victory and honor come from God alone. He is my refuge, a rock where no enemy can reach me. (NLT)

David prayed for safety from evil people, and we can do the same.

Psalm 140:1–6 O LORD, rescue me from evil people. Protect me from those who are violent, those who plot evil in their hearts and stir up trouble all day long. Their tongues sting like a snake; the venom of a viper drips from their lips. O LORD, keep me out of the hands of the wicked....The proud have set a trap to catch me; they have stretched out a net; they have placed traps all along the way. I said to the LORD, "You are my God!" Listen, O LORD, to my cries for mercy! (NLT)

Psalm 61:1–4 O God, listen to my cry! Hear my prayer! From the ends of the earth, I cry to you for help when my heart is over-whelmed. Lead me to the towering rock of safety, for you are my safe refuge, a fortress where my enemies cannot reach me. Let me live forever in your sanctuary, safe beneath the shelter of your wings! (NLT)

Do not allow past fears to control the present. When there is nothing we can do to correct the past, we must entrust it to God's care.

Isaiah 43:18–19 Forget the former things; do not dwell on the past. See, I am doing a new thing! Now it springs up; do you not perceive it? I am making a way in the wilderness and streams in the wasteland. (NIV)

Philippians 3:13–14 Brothers and sisters, I do not consider myself yet to have taken hold of it. But one thing I do: Forgetting what is behind and straining toward what is ahead, I press on toward the goal to win the prize for which God has called me heavenward in Christ Jesus. (NIV)

Matthew 10:26 But don't be afraid of those who threaten you. For the time is coming when everything that is covered will be revealed, and all that is secret will be made known to all. (NLT)

The God who is sovereign over our past can help us in the present.

Psalm 103:3–6, 8–11 He forgives all my sins and heals all my diseases. He redeems me from death and crowns me with love and tender mercies. He fills my life with good things. My youth is renewed like the eagle's! The LORD gives righteousness and justice to all who are treated unfairly. . . . The LORD is compassionate and merciful, slow to get angry and filled with unfailing love. He will not constantly accuse us, nor remain angry forever. He does not punish us for all our sins; he does not deal harshly with us, as we deserve. For his unfailing love toward those who fear him is as great as the height of the heavens above the earth. (NLT)

We can always talk to God about our problems.

Hebrews 4:16 Let us then with confidence draw near to the throne of grace, that we may receive mercy and find grace to help in time of need. (ESV)

Philippians 4:6–7 Don't worry about anything; instead, pray about everything. Tell God what you need, and thank him for all he has done. Then you will experience God's peace, which exceeds anything we can understand. His peace will guard your hearts and minds as you live in Christ Jesus. (NLT)

God is sufficient to give us strength in our trials.

2 Corinthians 12:9–10 But he said to me, "My grace is sufficient for you, for my power is made perfect in weakness." Therefore I will boast all the more gladly about my weaknesses, so that Christ's power may rest on me. That is why, for Christ's sake, I delight in weaknesses, in insults, in hardships, in persecutions, in difficulties. For when I am weak, then I am strong. (NIV)

God is our refuge, our strong protector.

Psalm 17:8–9 Guard me as you would guard your own eyes. Hide me in the shadow of your wings. Protect me from wicked people who attack me, from murderous enemies who surround me. (NLT)

Isaiah 25:4 But you are a tower of refuge to the poor, O Lord, a tower of refuge to the needy in distress. You are a refuge from the storm and a shelter from the heat. For the oppressive acts of ruthless people are like a storm beating against a wall. (NLT)

We can hope in a future day when God will redeem all things and there will be no more pain.

Revelation 21:1–5 Then I saw a new heaven and a new earth, for the first heaven and the first earth had passed away, and the sea was no more. And I saw the holy city, new Jerusalem, coming down out of heaven from God, prepared as a bride adorned for her husband. And I heard a loud voice from the throne saying, "Behold, the dwelling place of God is with man. He will dwell with them, and they will be his people, and God himself will be with them as their God. He will wipe away every tear from their eyes, and death shall be no more, neither shall there be mourning nor crying nor pain anymore, for the former things have passed away." (ESV)

Do not keep silent! If you are in a relationship that is in any way abusive, don't wait any longer. Immediately go to someone you trust for help. If you are not heard, do not give up—talk to someone wise until you find help. The most important thing is that you find assistance. Abuse is never an option.

PRACTICAL LIVING

- Read Appendix F, "Applying the Gospel to Daily Life for Those Abused."
- If you're in an abusive relationship, keep a record of events, what was said and done.
- Talk with a biblical counselor.
- Separate yourself from the situation. Seek a safe haven: a friend's home, a church, a women's shelter.
- Consider if a restraining order is necessary.
- Start a healing journal of prayers, Scripture, and forgiveness.
- See a physician.
- Talk to someone in a trusted community. There are many organizations that can be trusted to help women experiencing abuse, such as Focus Ministries or Safe Haven Ministries.
- See related topics: Hope, Self-Worth, Grief, and Difficult Memories.

RECOMMENDED READING

- *Rid of My Disgrace: Hope and Healing for Victims of Sexual Assault.* Justin Holcomb and Lindsey Holcomb. Crossway.

- *Walking with God through Pain and Suffering*. Tim Keller. Penguin.
- *Is It My Fault? Hope and Healing for Those Suffering Domestic Violence*. Lindsey A. Holcomb. Moody.
- *Sexual Abuse: Beauty for Ashes*. Robert Kellemen. P&R.
- *Emotionally Destructive Relationships*. Leslie Vernick. Harvest House.
- *Finding God in the Ruins*. Matt Bays. David C. Cook.
- *Suffering and the Heart of God*. Diane Langberg. New Growth.

· Addiction ·

A counterfeit god is anything so central and essential to your life that, should you lose it, your life would feel hardly worth living. An idol has such a controlling position in your heart that you can spend most of your passion and energy, your emotional and financial resources, on it without a second thought.[1]

Tim Keller

Sinful patterns are extremely dangerous and take away from our relationship with God.

Romans 6:12–14 Do not let sin control the way you live; do not give in to sinful desires. Do not let any part of your body become an instrument of evil to serve sin. Instead, give yourselves completely to God, for you were dead, but now you have new life. So use your whole body as an instrument to do what is right for the glory of God. Sin is no longer your master, for you no longer live under the requirements of the law. Instead, you live under the freedom of God's grace. (NLT)

Romans 13:13–14 Let us conduct ourselves properly, as people who live in the light of day—no orgies or drunkenness, no immorality or indecency, no fighting or jealousy. But take up the weapons of the Lord Jesus Christ, and stop paying attention to your sinful nature and satisfying its desires. (GNT)

. . . .

Addiction is—like all sin—a form of idolatry because it elevates some proximate good to the status of ultimate good, a status that belongs to God alone. But addiction is uniquely alluring, uniquely captivating, and uniquely powerful because its object comes so close to making good on its false promise to be God. All sin is an attempt to overreach our powers and to establish on our own a flourishing and fulfillment that can only be found within right relationship to God.[2]

Kent Dunnington

. . . .

Develop a relationship with God, not with harmful substitutes.

Ephesians 5:18 Do not get drunk with wine, which will only ruin you; instead, be filled with the Spirit. (GNT)

Addiction to anything can damage our bodies.

 1 Corinthians 6:19 Or do you not know that your body is a temple of the Holy Spirit who is in you, whom you have from God, and that you are not your own? (NASB)

An idolatrous attachment can lead you to break any promise, rationalize any indiscretion, or betray any other allegiance, in order to hold on to it. It may drive you to violate all good and proper boundaries. To practice idolatry is to be a slave.[3]

Tim Keller

There is escape available from addiction. These habits can be changed.

2 Corinthians 5:17–18 This means that anyone who belongs to Christ has become a new person. The old life is gone; a new life has begun! And all of this is a gift from God, who brought us back to himself through Christ. (NLT)

Colossians 1:13–14 He rescued us from the power of darkness and brought us safe into the kingdom of his dear Son, by whom we are set free, that is, our sins are forgiven. (GNT)

1 Corinthians 6:9–11 Or do you not know that the unrighteous will not inherit the kingdom of God? Do not be deceived: neither the sexually immoral, nor idolaters, nor adulterers, nor men who practice homosexuality, nor thieves, nor the greedy, nor drunkards, nor revilers, nor swindlers will inherit the kingdom of God. And such were some of you. But you were washed, you were sanctified, you were justified in the name of the Lord Jesus Christ and by the Spirit of our God. (ESV)

PRACTICAL LIVING

- Listen to Tim Keller's sermons "How Sin Makes Us Addicts" and "Removing Idols of the Heart," available online at GospelInLife.com.

- Read the book *The Power of Habit* by Charles Duhigg. Determine your "keystone habits" to help you make changes.
- Consider seeing a physician and counselor.
- Become involved in *Steps: A Gospel-Centered Recovery Program* (available at Lifeway.com).
- Ask yourself why you have a relationship with this addiction. Why is it so important?
- How does Ephesians 5:18 apply to you? What or who do you allow control over you?
- Relationships may need to change. Cut off the old; replace with the positive. See Ephesians 4:17–32.
- Develop a support system. Find someone to help hold you accountable: in finances, behaviors, habits, and routines.
- Stay away from places of temptation.
- Read Psalm 107 daily. The goodness of God surpasses all.
- See related section: Knowing God.

RECOMMENDED READING

- *Counterfeit Gods.* Tim Keller. Penguin.
- *The Power of Habit.* Charles Duhigg. Random House.
- *Addictions.* Ed Welch. P&R.
- *Divine Intervention: Hope and Help for Families of Addicts.* Mark Shaw. Focus.

· Adultery ·

Adultery is any physical or emotional attachment or behavior with someone other than your spouse or with someone else's spouse. Physical and emotional adultery includes thoughts, touching, intercourse, or bonding with another person through close friendship and intimate communication, even when no physical boundaries are crossed. If you've committed adultery or have been wronged in this way by your spouse, Jesus offers hope and forgiveness.

Adultery is not a gray area. God absolutely and specifically commands you not to do it. No situations exist in which adultery is justified.

Exodus 20:14 You shall not commit adultery. (NKJV)

Romans 13:9 For the commandments say, "You must not commit adultery. You must not murder. You must not steal. You must not covet." These—and other such commandments—are summed up in this one commandment: "Love your neighbor as yourself." (NLT)

Another person's spouse is off-limits. You have no right to separate what God has placed together.

Mark 10:8–9 "And the two shall become one flesh." So they are no longer two but one flesh. What therefore God has joined together, let not man separate. (ESV)

1 Thessalonians 4:6–7 Never harm or cheat a fellow believer in this matter by violating his wife, for the Lord avenges all such sins, as we have solemnly warned you before. God has called us to live holy lives, not impure lives. (NLT)

Exodus 20:17 You shall not covet your neighbor's house; you shall not covet your neighbor's wife, or his male servant, or his female servant, or his ox, or his donkey, or anything that is your neighbor's. (ESV)

Lustful thinking—imagining what it would be like to be with someone else—is mental and emotional adultery.

Matthew 5:28 But I say to you that everyone who looks at a woman with lustful intent has already committed adultery with her in his heart. (ESV)

Adultery, like all sin, separates us from God. Only Jesus Christ offers us freedom.

1 Corinthians 6:9–11 Do you not know that the unrighteous will not inherit the kingdom of God? Do not be deceived: neither the sexually immoral, nor idolaters, nor adulterers, nor men who practice homosexuality, nor thieves, nor the greedy, nor drunkards, nor revilers, nor swindlers will inherit the kingdom of God. And such were some of you. But you were washed, you were sanctified, you were justified in the name of the Lord Jesus Christ and by the Spirit of our God. (ESV)

Adultery is stopped by changing our thinking and seeing it as sin.

Romans 8:5–6 Those who are dominated by the sinful nature think about sinful things, but those who are controlled by the Holy Spirit think about things that please the Spirit. So letting your sinful nature control your mind leads to death. But letting the Spirit control your mind leads to life and peace. (NLT)

Romans 12:2 Do not conform to the pattern of this world, but be transformed by the renewing of your mind. Then you will be able to test and approve what God's will is—his good, pleasing and perfect will. (NIV)

Adultery always has real consequences which lead to destruction.

Proverbs 6:27–29, 32 Can a man carry fire next to his chest and his clothes not be burned? Or can one walk on hot coals and his feet not be scorched? So is he who goes in to his neighbor's wife; none who touches her will go unpunished. . . . He who commits adultery lacks sense; he who does it destroys himself. (ESV)

Proverbs 5:20–23 Why, my son, be intoxicated with another man's wife? Why embrace the bosom of a wayward woman? For your ways are in full view of the LORD, and he examines all your paths. The evil deeds of the wicked ensnare them; the cords of their sins hold them fast. For lack of discipline they will die, led astray by their own great folly. (NIV)

Steps that help protect against adultery:

Self-control

 1 Thessalonians 4:3–5 God's will is for you to be holy, so stay away from all sexual sin. Then each of you will control his own body and live in holiness and honor—not in lustful passion like the pagans who do not know God and his ways. (NLT)

God's wisdom in his Word

Proverbs 2:16–18 Wisdom will save you also from the adulterous woman, from the wayward woman with her seductive words, who has left the partner of her youth and ignored the covenant she made before God. Surely her house leads down to death and her paths to the spirits of the dead. (NIV)

A healthy sexual relationship within marriage

1 Corinthians 7:2–5 But because there is so much sexual immorality, each man should have his own wife, and each woman should have her own husband. The husband should fulfill his wife's sexual needs, and the wife should fulfill her husband's needs. The wife gives authority over her body to her husband, and the husband gives authority over his body to his wife. Do not deprive each other of sexual relations, unless you both agree to refrain from sexual intimacy for a limited time so you can give yourselves more completely to prayer. Afterward, you should come together again so that Satan won't be able to tempt you because of your lack of self-control. (NLT)

If you fall into this sin, confess, repent, and seek God's forgiveness and restoration with your spouse.

1 John 1:9 If we confess our sins, He is faithful and just to forgive us our sins and to cleanse us from all unrighteousness. (NKJV)

Psalm 32:1–5 Blessed is the one whose transgression is forgiven, whose sin is covered. Blessed is the man against whom the LORD counts no iniquity, and in whose spirit there is no deceit. For when I kept silent, my bones wasted away through my groaning all day long. For day and night your hand was heavy upon me; my strength was dried up as by the heat of summer. I acknowledged my sin to you, and I did not cover my iniquity; I said, "I will confess my transgressions to the LORD," and you forgave the iniquity of my sin. (ESV)

PRACTICAL LIVING

- Create a plan—how do you protect your marriage and encourage faithfulness?
- If your spouse has failed in this area, watch the video seminar "True Betrayal: Overcoming the Betrayal of Your

Spouse's Sexual Sin" (available online at BradHambrick.
com/TrueBetrayal).

- Seek wise counsel—whether a trusted friend, pastor, or a
  biblical counselor or therapist. Talk to someone you can trust.
- If you've failed in this area, rededicate yourself to your re-
  lationship with God and others through purity, forgiveness,
  and change.
- Pray daily for the restoration of your marriage.
- See related topics: Grief, Hope, Trials, Comfort, Forgiving
  Others, and the Knowing God section.

RECOMMENDED READING

- *The Meaning of Marriage.* Tim and Kathy Keller. Penguin.
- *How to Act Right When Your Spouse Acts Wrong.* Leslie
  Vernick. WaterBrook.
- *How to Save Your Marriage Alone.* Ed Wheat. Zondervan.
- *Heart Broken and Healing* (workbook). Mary Asher. Focus.

· Death ·

But let me tell you something wonderful, a mystery I'll probably
never fully understand. . . . On signal from that trumpet from
heaven, the dead will be up and out of their graves, beyond the reach
of death, never to die again. . . . Then the saying will come true:
Death swallowed by triumphant Life! Who got the last word, oh,

Death? Oh, Death, who's afraid of you now? It was sin that made death so frightening and law-code guilt that gave sin its leverage, its destructive power. But now in a single victorious stroke of Life, all three—sin, guilt, death—are gone, the gift of our Master, Jesus Christ. Thank God! (1 Corinthians 15:51–57 MSG)

Death does not separate us from God and his love.

Romans 8:38–39 For I am sure that neither death nor life, nor angels nor rulers, nor things present nor things to come, nor powers, nor height nor depth, nor anything else in all creation, will be able to separate us from the love of God in Christ Jesus our Lord. (ESV)

Psalm 23:4 Even though I walk through the valley of the shadow of death, I will fear no evil, for you are with me; your rod and your staff, they comfort me. (ESV)

Death for the believer means being in the presence of Christ.

Philippians 1:21–24 For to me, to live is Christ and to die is gain. If I am to go on living in the body, this will mean fruitful labor for me. Yet what shall I choose? I do not know! I am torn between the two: I desire to depart and be with Christ, which is better by far; but it is more necessary for you that I remain in the body. (NIV)

Death for a believer means receiving a new body.

Philippians 3:21 He will change our weak mortal bodies and make them like his own glorious body, using that power by which he is able to bring all things under his rule. (GNT)

1 Corinthians 15:52–53 It will happen in a moment, in the blink of an eye, when the last trumpet is blown. For when the trumpet sounds, those who have died will be raised to live forever. And we who are living will also be transformed. For our dying bodies must

be transformed into bodies that will never die; our mortal bodies must be transformed into immortal bodies. (NLT)

Jesus's death on the cross removes all our fear of death.

Hebrews 2:9–10, 14–15 But we do see Jesus, who was made lower than the angels for a little while, now crowned with glory and honor because he suffered death, so that by the grace of God he might taste death for everyone. In bringing many sons and daughters to glory, it was fitting that God, for whom and through whom everything exists, should make the pioneer of their salvation perfect through what he suffered. . . . Since the children have flesh and blood, he too shared in their humanity so that by his death he might destroy the power of him who holds the power of death—that is, the devil—and free those who all their lives were held in slavery by their fear of death. (NIV)

God's strength is always available.

 Isaiah 41:10 Do not fear, for I am with you; do not anxiously look about you, for I am your God. I will strengthen you, surely I will help you, surely I will uphold you with My righteous right hand. (NASB)

Lamentations 3:21–24 This I recall to my mind, therefore I have hope. The LORD's lovingkindnesses indeed never cease, for His compassions never fail. They are new every morning; great is Your faithfulness. "The LORD is my portion," says my soul, "therefore I have hope in Him." (NASB)

Loss is real, but we can express our grief to God.

Psalm 31:9–10 Be merciful to me, LORD, for I am in trouble; my eyes are tired from so much crying; I am completely worn out. I am exhausted by sorrow, and weeping has shortened my life. I am weak from all my troubles; even my bones are wasting away. (GNT)

Psalm 145:18–19 The LORD is near to all who call on him, to all who call on him in truth. He fulfills the desire of those who fear him; he also hears their cry and saves them. (ESV)

God cares for us and understands the brokenhearted. He can use our loss to bring us closer to himself.

Psalm 34:18 The LORD is near to the brokenhearted and saves the crushed in spirit. (ESV)

Psalm 147:3 He heals the brokenhearted and binds up their wounds. (ESV)

Matthew 5:4 Blessed are those who mourn, for they shall be comforted. (ESV)

John 14:27 Peace I leave with you; my peace I give to you. Not as the world gives do I give to you. Let not your hearts be troubled, neither let them be afraid. (ESV)

There is hope for the future after death.

Revelation 21:3–4 I heard a loud shout from the throne, say-ing, "Look, God's home is now among his people! He will live with them, and they will be his people. God himself will be with them. He will wipe every tear from their eyes, and there will be no more death or sorrow or crying or pain. All these things are gone forever." (NLT)

God can restore our lost joy.

Isaiah 51:11 Those who have been ransomed by the LORD will return. They will enter Jerusalem singing, crowned with everlasting joy. Sorrow and mourning will disappear, and they will be filled with joy and gladness. (NLT)

Isaiah 61:1–3 The Spirit of the Lord GOD is upon me, because
the LORD has anointed me to bring good news to the poor; he has
sent me to bind up the brokenhearted, to proclaim liberty to the
captives, and the opening of the prison to those who are bound; to
proclaim the year of the LORD's favor, and the day of vengeance of
our God; to comfort all who mourn; to grant to those who mourn
in Zion—to give them a beautiful headdress instead of ashes, the
oil of gladness instead of mourning, the garment of praise instead
of a faint spirit; that they may be called oaks of righteousness, the
planting of the LORD, that he may be glorified. (ESV)

PRACTICAL LIVING

- Read and reread these Psalms of comfort: 34; 42; 46; 139;
  143; and 145. Select special verses; write them out, and place
  them in strategic locations around your house.
- Keep a list of memories you treasure and add to it often.
- Find one person who will commit to calling you each day for
  encouragement. Call them when you need to talk.
- Reach out to others who have experienced loss through death.
- Plan special times on birthdays and holidays.
- See related topics: Worry, Grief, and Hope.

RECOMMENDED READING

- *A Severe Mercy*. Sheldon Van Auken. HarperOne.
- *The Problem of Pain*. C. S. Lewis. HarperOne.
- *A Grief Observed*. C. S. Lewis. HarperOne.
- *One Minute After You Die*. Erwin Lutzer. Moody.
- *The Glory of Heaven*. John MacArthur. Crossway.
- *Facing Death with Hope* (booklet). David Powlison. CCEF.
- *Heaven*. Randy Alcorn. Tyndale.

· Death of a Child ·

God is our anchor and our hope in this sadness.

Hebrews 6:18–20 So God has given both his promise and his oath. These two things are unchangeable because it is impossible for God to lie. Therefore, we who have fled to him for refuge can have great confidence as we hold to the hope that lies before us. This hope is a strong and trustworthy anchor for our souls. It leads us through the curtain into God's inner sanctuary. (NLT)

Children are precious, whether born or unborn.

Jeremiah 1:4–5 Now the word of the LORD came to me, saying, "Before I formed you in the womb I knew you, and before you were born I consecrated you; I appointed you a prophet to the nations." (ESV)

Psalm 139:13–15 You created every part of me; you put me together in my mother's womb. I praise you because you are to be feared; all you do is strange and wonderful. I know it with all my heart. When my bones were being formed, carefully put together in my mother's womb, when I was growing there in secret, you knew that I was there. (GNT)

God understands our grief and his heart is tender.

Psalm 147:3 He heals the brokenhearted and binds up their wounds. (ESV)

Psalm 40:1–2 I waited patiently for the LORD to help me, and he turned to me and heard my cry. He lifted me out of the pit of despair, out of the mud and the mire. He set my feet on solid ground and steadied me as I walked along. (NLT)

Psalm 18:1–6 I love you, Lᴏʀᴅ, my strength. The Lᴏʀᴅ is my rock, my fortress and my deliverer; my God is my rock, in whom I take refuge, my shield and the horn of my salvation, my stronghold. I called to the Lᴏʀᴅ, who is worthy of praise, and I have been saved from my enemies. The cords of death entangled me; the torrents of destruction overwhelmed me. The cords of the grave coiled around me; the snares of death confronted me. In my distress I called to the Lᴏʀᴅ; I cried to my God for help. From his temple he heard my voice; my cry came before him, into his ears. (NIV)

Isaiah 25:8 He will swallow up death for all time, and the Lord Gᴏᴅ will wipe tears away from all faces, and He will remove the reproach of His people from all the earth; for the Lᴏʀᴅ has spoken. (NASB)

2 Corinthians 1:3–4 All praise to God, the Father of our Lord Jesus Christ. God is our merciful Father and the source of all comfort. He comforts us in all our troubles so that we can comfort others. When they are troubled, we will be able to give them the same comfort God has given us. (NLT)

During difficult times, we can depend on God's sovereignty.

Psalm 18:30 This God—his way is perfect; the word of the Lᴏʀᴅ proves true; he is a shield for all those who take refuge in him. (ESV)

Psalm 69:29–30 I am suffering and in pain. Rescue me, O God, by your saving power. Then I will praise God's name with singing, and I will honor him with thanksgiving. (NLT)

Psalm 90:1–2 Lord, You have been our dwelling place in all generations. Before the mountains were born or You gave birth to the earth and the world, even from everlasting to everlasting, You are God. (NASB)

 Psalm 91:1–2 He who dwells in the shelter of the Most High will abide in the shadow of the Almighty. I will say to the Lᴏʀᴅ, "My refuge and my fortress, my God, in whom I trust!" (NASB)

Ecclesiastes 11:5 As you do not know the way the spirit comes to the bones in the womb of a woman with child, so you do not know the work of God who makes everything. (ESV)

Isaiah 44:24 This is what the LORD says—your Redeemer and Creator: I am the LORD, who made all things. I alone stretched out the heavens. Who was with me when I made the earth? (NLT)

Job 42:2 I know that you can do all things; no purpose of yours can be thwarted. (NIV)

. . . .

At this stage of our grief, I am starting to feel like we are on a mountaintop looking down into a city called Grief. The city was dim during deep grief but now, we are seeing street lights come on. Each light post represents a person who was touched by our grief for the Glory of God. Would I change our walk and have Simon here? Some days it's a yes. Without question. While other days it's a no . . . which makes me cry, but it's true. I can wait to hold Simon and Thomas again for eternity if it's going to bring more family, friends, and strangers into the Kingdom with Christ.[1]

Amy Balentine

. . . .

Have hope in the future resurrection of your child.

1 Thessalonians 4:13–14, 16–18 But we do not want you to be uninformed, brothers, about those who are asleep, that you may not grieve as others do who have no hope. For since we believe that Jesus died and rose again, even so, through Jesus, God will bring with him those who have fallen asleep. . . . For the Lord himself will descend from heaven with a cry of command, with the voice of an archangel, and with the sound of the trumpet of God. And the dead in Christ will rise first. Then we who are alive, who are left, will be caught up together with them in the clouds to meet the

Lord in the air, and so we will always be with the Lord. Therefore
encourage one another with these words. (ESV)

PRACTICAL LIVING

- Journey with Amy Balentine as she walks through grief and
joy in the loss of her two sons, Simon and Thomas (http://
www.balentinememoirs.com/).
- Encourage someone who has experienced the death of their
child. Purchase a soft household afghan or blanket and include a card with a version of the following: "Why a blanket? I wanted you to have something cozy and tangible that
represents the verse Psalm 91:4, 'He will cover you with his
wings; you will be safe in his care; his faithfulness will protect
and defend you'" (GNT).
- Miscarriage: To help with the grieving process, name your
baby, no matter how young.
- Honor your baby or child's memory—a plaque or painting
in your home, a special piece of jewelry, planting a tree or
garden.
- Make a scrapbook or keepsake box of the time you had with
your baby or child (cards, ultrasounds, baby's name, pictures,
special outfit or toys), to honor the memory of your child.
- Stillbirth: Hold the baby for a time after the birth. Depending on the age at delivery, take photos, plan a small funeral
or memorial.
- Seek out mentors or a support group who have walked this
same path. Let them pray with you and encourage you.
- If you have other children, be sure to gently help them
through the grief process as well.
- See related topics: Grief, Death, and Hope.

RECOMMENDED READING

- *Safe in the Arms of God.* John MacArthur. Thomas Nelson.
- "The Truth about Grief: What I Wish I Had Known When I Started My Grief Journey." Abby Rike. (Available online at RockThis.org.)
- "The Pain Receded and We Carry It Together." Shauna Niequist. (Available online at ShaunaNiequist.com.)
- "What Might Have Been" in *Bittersweet.* Shauna Niequist. Zondervan.
- *Free to Grieve.* Maureen Park. Bethany House.
- *Morning Will Come.* Sandy Day. Focus.
- *When Life Is Changed Forever.* Rick Taylor. Harvest House.
- *Grieving the Child I Never Knew.* Kathe Wunnenberg. Zondervan.

· Divorce ·

When we walk down the aisle, divorce is not something we're thinking about. A wedding day is full of hope and expectations. Yet still, so many marriages end in divorce. Our hopes crash headlong into the reality of unmet expectations and unrealized dreams. This is the sad reality of our broken world: divorce does happen, even to Christians. This topic is controversial; Bible scholars have different conclusions, especially about the question of remarriage. But the Bible is especially clear that no matter the issues in the marriage, the goal must first and foremost be to seek restoration, saving the marriage. Divorce is a last resort. (However, if you are in an abusive marriage, and/or if you or your children are in danger, please seek help immediately.)

Marriage is a sacred binding covenant; God created it to last.

Genesis 2:22–25 The Lord God fashioned into a woman the rib which He had taken from the man, and brought her to the man. The man said, "This is now bone of my bones, and flesh of my flesh; she shall be called Woman, because she was taken out of Man." For this reason a man shall leave his father and his mother, and be joined to his wife; and they shall become one flesh. And the man and his wife were both naked and were not ashamed. (NASB)

 Matthew 19:6 So they are no longer two, but one flesh. What therefore God has joined together, let no man separate. (NASB)

God allowed divorce because of the hardness of Israel's heart.

Matthew 19:3–9 And Pharisees came up to him and tested him by asking, "Is it lawful to divorce one's wife for any cause?" He answered, "Have you not read that he who created them from the beginning made them male and female, and said, 'Therefore a man shall leave his father and his mother and hold fast to his wife, and the two shall become one flesh'? So they are no longer two but one flesh. What therefore God has joined together, let not man separate." They said to him, "Why then did Moses command one to give a certificate of divorce and to send her away?" He said to them, "Because of your hardness of heart Moses allowed you to divorce your wives, but from the beginning it was not so." (ESV)

God hates divorce and expects marriage to be a faithful
commitment.

Malachi 2:14–16 You cry out, "Why doesn't the Lord accept my
worship?" I'll tell you why! Because the Lord witnessed the vows
you and your wife made when you were young. But you have been
unfaithful to her, though she remained your faithful partner, the
wife of your marriage vows. Didn't the Lord make you one with
your wife? In body and spirit you are his. And what does he want?
Godly children from your union. So guard your heart; remain loyal
to the wife of your youth. "For I hate divorce!" says the Lord,
the God of Israel. "To divorce your wife is to overwhelm her with
cruelty," says the Lord of Heaven's Armies. "So guard your heart;
do not be unfaithful to your wife." (NLT)

Having a spouse who is an unbeliever is not a reason
for divorce.

1 Corinthians 7:12–13 To the rest I say this (I, not the Lord):
If any brother has a wife who is not a believer and she is willing
to live with him, he must not divorce her. And if a woman has a
husband who is not a believer and he is willing to live with her, she
must not divorce him. (NIV)

Whatever the problems in a marriage, reconciliation and
restoration is always the goal.

1 Corinthians 7:10–11 To the married I give this command (not
I, but the Lord): A wife must not separate from her husband. But if
she does, she must remain unmarried or else be reconciled to her
husband. And a husband must not divorce his wife. (NIV)

Hebrews 12:14–15 Make every effort to live in peace with
everyone and to be holy; without holiness no one will see the Lord.
See to it that no one falls short of the grace of God and that no
bitter root grows up to cause trouble and defile many. (NIV)

God allows divorce when there has been unfaithfulness and/or desertion by an unbelieving spouse. However, seeking reconciliation is always the goal.

Matthew 5:31–32 It has been said, "Anyone who divorces his wife must give her a certificate of divorce." But I tell you that anyone who divorces his wife, except for sexual immorality, makes her the victim of adultery, and anyone who marries the divorced woman commits adultery. (NIV)

If divorce does happen, remarriage after divorce is biblically acceptable in three situations:

If the divorce took place before the person became a believer

2 Corinthians 5:17 Therefore, if anyone is in Christ, he is a new creation; old things have passed away; behold, all things have become new. (NKJV)

If the divorce happened because of the unrepentant unfaithfulness of the spouse

Matthew 19:9 I tell you that anyone who divorces his wife, except for sexual immorality, and marries another woman commits adultery. (NIV)

If an unbelieving spouse deserts a believing spouse

1 Corinthians 7:15 But if the unbeliever leaves, let it be so. The brother or the sister is not bound in such circumstances; God has called us to live in peace. (NIV)

PRACTICAL LIVING

- Study the article "A Summary of Questions to Ask on Divorce and Remarriage" by Justin Taylor (available online at TheGospelCoalition.org).
- Research the top reasons why people divorce. Construct a plan to prevent these in your marriage.
- Seek intensive, biblical counseling to reconcile and restore your marriage when possible.
- See related topics: Decision Making, Hope, Trials, Contentment, Disappointment, and Marriage.

RECOMMENDED READING

- *Marriage, Divorce, and Remarriage in the Bible*. Jay Adams. Zondervan.
- *The Meaning of Marriage*. Tim and Kathy Keller. Penguin.
- *Divorce*. Charles Swindoll. Multnomah.
- *The Divorce Dilemma*. John MacArthur. Day One.
- *I Don't Want a Divorce*. David Clarke. Revell.

· Eating Struggles ·

We need to understand that the whole arena of food and eating is simply a mirror of the heart.[1]

Penny Orr

Our trust, success, and security are not in our bodies. Rather, our hope is in our Maker and through Jesus's work on the cross.

Philippians 3:8–9 Yes, all the things I once thought were so important are gone from my life. Compared to the high privilege of knowing Christ Jesus as my Master, firsthand, everything I once thought I had going for me is insignificant. . . . I've dumped it all in the trash so that I could embrace Christ and be embraced by him. I didn't want some petty, inferior brand of righteousness that comes from keeping a list of rules when I could get the robust kind that comes from trusting Christ—God's righteousness. (MSG)

Psalm 62:5–8 For God alone, O my soul, wait in silence, for my hope is from him. He only is my rock and my salvation, my fortress; I shall not be shaken. On God rests my salvation and my glory; my mighty rock, my refuge is God. Trust in him at all times, O people; pour out your heart before him; God is a refuge for us. (ESV)

God loves me—because he made me. And even more, because he died for me. And suddenly my body was no longer just skin covering muscle covering bone. It was a vessel, and

God wanted to pour his love into me so I could pour it into others. We are not just physical beings. We are spiritual, and part
of me always knew this, and this is why food was never enough.[2]

Emily Wierenga

. . . .

There is hope for overcoming this struggle.

Psalm 107:17–22 Some of you were sick because you'd lived a
bad life, your bodies feeling the effects of your sin; You couldn't
stand the sight of food, so miserable you thought you'd be better
off dead. Then you called out to GOD in your desperate condition;
he got you out in the nick of time. He spoke the word that healed
you, that pulled you back from the brink of death. So thank GOD
for his marvelous love, for his miracle mercy to the children he loves;
Offer thanksgiving sacrifices, tell the world what he's done—sing
it out! (MSG)

Lamentations 3:21–23 This I recall to my mind, therefore I
have hope. The LORD's lovingkindnesses indeed never cease, for
His compassions never fail. They are new every morning; great is
Your faithfulness. (NASB)

Our bodies belong to God and exist for his glory.

Psalm 139:13–14 You made all the delicate, inner parts of my
body and knit me together in my mother's womb. Thank you
for making me so wonderfully complex! Your workmanship is
marvelous—how well I know it. (NLT)

1 Corinthians 6:19–20 Or do you not know that your body is a
temple of the Holy Spirit who is in you, whom you have from God,
and that you are not your own? For you have been bought with a
price: therefore glorify God in your body. (NASB)

1 Corinthians 10:31 Whether, then, you eat or drink or whatever
you do, do all to the glory of God. (NASB)

We are to choose to give our bodies back to God, following his way and not our own.

> Romans 12:1–2 And so, dear brothers and sisters, I plead with you to give your bodies to God because of all he has done for you. Let them be a living and holy sacrifice—the kind he will find acceptable. This is truly the way to worship him. Don't copy the behavior and customs of this world, but let God transform you into a new person by changing the way you think. Then you will learn to know God's will for you, which is good and pleasing and perfect. (NLT)

Trying to control what belongs to God is sin. Obsessing about self is idolatry.

> Colossians 3:5 Put to death therefore what is earthly in you: sexual immorality, impurity, passion, evil desire, and covetousness, which is idolatry. (ESV)

> 1 John 1:8–9 If we say we have no sin, we deceive ourselves, and the truth is not in us. If we confess our sins, he is faithful and just to forgive us our sins and to cleanse us from all unrighteousness. (ESV)

· ·

If we're forced to deny our sin from the day we're born, we'll never realize we need a Savior. We'll only ever punish ourselves for not being what we feel we're supposed to be: perfect.[3]

Emily Wierenga

· ·

In order to overcome eating struggles, we must change our thinking.

> Isaiah 55:8–9 For my thoughts are not your thoughts, neither are your ways my ways, declares the LORD. For as the heavens are

higher than the earth, so are my ways higher than your ways and my thoughts than your thoughts. (ESV)

Philippians 4:8 Finally, brothers and sisters, whatever is true, whatever is noble, whatever is right, whatever is pure, whatever is lovely, whatever is admirable—if anything is excellent or praiseworthy—think about such things. (NIV)

· ·

God calls us to something greater than a life of balancing scales; God calls us to place the full weight of our struggles on the promises of Scripture. In God, we are more than any number—either our weight or our grade-point averages—can define.[4]

Melissa Steffan

· ·

Pray before eating; give thanks for the food God has provided.

 1 Timothy 4:4–5 Since everything God created is good, we should not reject any of it but receive it with thanks. For we know it is made acceptable by the word of God and prayer. (NLT)

1 Timothy 6:17 Instruct those who are rich in this present world not to be conceited or to fix their hope on the uncertainty of riches, but on God, who richly supplies us with all things to enjoy. (NASB)

Gluttony is not seen favorably in Scripture.

Proverbs 23:20–21 Do not join those who drink too much wine or gorge themselves on meat, for drunkards and gluttons become poor, and drowsiness clothes them in rags. (NIV)

Proverbs 28:7 The one who keeps the law is a son with understanding, but a companion of gluttons shames his father. (ESV)

PRACTICAL LIVING

• Study the chart "Religion vs. The Gospel" by Tim Keller (available online at dbcu.org). Evaluate how the way you eat is controlled by religion and/or the gospel.

• Eating struggles are symptoms of heart struggles and not really about food. What are you trying to control? Why are you anxious? What do you fear?

• Memorize Psalm 139:14.

• Practice honesty. Seek accountability. No lying about eating.

• Keep a food journal that can be reviewed by a mentor. Include water and supplements.

• Talk often with a trusted Christian or counselor.

• Eat healthy food. Meet with a nutritionist.

• Be evaluated by your physician.

• See related topics: Addiction, Hope, Worry, Self-Worth, Guilt, Pride, Trust, and the section on Knowing God.

RECOMMENDED READING

• *The Story of God's Love for You*. Sally Lloyd-Jones. Zondervan.

• *Love to Eat. Hate to Eat*. Elyse Fitzpatrick. Harvest House.

• *Counterfeit Gods*. Tim Keller. Penguin.

• *The Prodigal God*. Tim Keller. Penguin.

• *Uncommon Vessels: A Program for Developing Godly Eating Habits*. Elyse Fitzpatrick. Harvest House.

• "Help for Habitual Overeaters" in *Women Counseling Women*. Elyse Fitzpatrick. Harvest House.

· Illness ·

In Jesus, the good physician, we might not find the answers we're seeking, but we find comfort for today and hope beyond the grave. In his life, we remember he was no stranger to emotional heartache and physical pain. In his Word, we know these light and momentary afflictions are nothing compared to the future glory that will be revealed (2 Cor. 4:17). And in his promises, we take hope that all broken things—even our sore, brittle bodies—will be made new and whole again, and pain will finally be a distant memory.[1]

Jeremy Linneman

God doesn't always take away our suffering, but he gives us enough grace to see us through suffering.

2 Corinthians 12:8–10 Three different times I begged the Lord to take it away. Each time he said, "My grace is all you need. My power works best in weakness." So now I am glad to boast about my weaknesses, so that the power of Christ can work through me. That's why I take pleasure in my weaknesses, and in the insults, hardships, persecutions, and troubles that I suffer for Christ. For when I am weak, then I am strong. (NLT)

Psalm 119:71 My suffering was good for me, for it taught me to pay attention to your decrees. (NLT)

We never face health problems alone.

 Isaiah 41:10 Fear not, for I am with you; be not dismayed, for I am your God; I will strengthen you, I will help you, I will uphold you with my righteous right hand. (ESV)

Philippians 4:19 And my God will supply all your needs according to His riches in glory in Christ Jesus. (NASB)

2 Corinthians 4:16 Therefore we do not lose heart. Though outwardly we are wasting away, yet inwardly we are being renewed day by day. (NIV)

God provides strength.

2 Samuel 22:33 This God is my strong refuge and has made my way blameless. (ESV)

Psalm 73:26 My flesh and my heart may fail, but God is the strength of my heart and my portion forever. (ESV)

Isaiah 40:30–31 Even youths shall faint and be weary, and young men shall fall exhausted; but they who wait for the Lord shall renew their strength; they shall mount up with wings like eagles; they shall run and not be weary; they shall walk and not faint. (ESV)

Focus on spiritual health.

Proverbs 3:1–2 My child, never forget the things I have taught you. Store my commands in your heart. If you do this, you will live many years, and your life will be satisfying. (NLT)

Proverbs 3:7–8 Do not be wise in your own eyes; fear the Lord and turn away from evil. It will be healing to your body and refreshment to your bones. (NASB)

Focus on emotional health.

Proverbs 14:30 A heart at peace gives life to the body, but envy rots the bones. (NIV)

Proverbs 18:14 The human spirit can endure a sick body, but who can bear a crushed spirit? (NLT)

Proverbs 17:22 A cheerful heart is good medicine, but a broken spirit saps a person's strength. (NLT)

The probability of health problems is a part of life.

2 Corinthians 5:4 While we live in these earthly bodies, we groan and sigh, but it's not that we want to die and get rid of these bodies that clothe us. Rather, we want to put on our new bodies so that these dying bodies will be swallowed up by life. (NLT)

Romans 8:23 And we believers also groan . . . for we long for our bodies to be released from sin and suffering. We, too, wait with eager hope for the day when God will give us our full rights as his adopted children, including the new bodies he has promised us. (NLT)

Illness, as a trial, develops character.

James 1:2–4 Consider it pure joy, my brothers and sisters, whenever you face trials of many kinds, because you know that the testing of your faith produces perseverance. Let perseverance finish its work so that you may be mature and complete, not lacking anything. (NIV)

Job 23:8–10 Behold, I go forward but He is not there, and backward, but I cannot perceive Him; when He acts on the left, I cannot behold Him; He turns on the right, I cannot see Him. But He knows the way I take; when He has tried me, I shall come forth as gold. (NASB)

Whatever health issues we face now, perfect health awaits the believer in heaven.

Revelation 21:4 And He will wipe away every tear from their eyes; and there will no longer be any death; there will no longer be any mourning, or crying, or pain; the first things have passed away. (NASB)

Philippians 3:20–21 But our citizenship is in heaven, and from it we await a Savior, the Lord Jesus Christ, who will transform our lowly body to be like his glorious body, by the power that enables him even to subject all things to himself. (ESV)

1 Corinthians 15:54–57 Then the saying will come true: Death swallowed by triumphant Life! Who got the last word, oh, Death? Oh, Death, who's afraid of you now? It was sin that made death so frightening and law-code guilt that gave sin its leverage, its destructive power. But now in a single victorious stroke of Life, all three—sin, guilt, death—are gone, the gift of our Master, Jesus Christ. Thank God! (MSG)

PRACTICAL LIVING

- Have regular appointments with physicians and keep all records and progress reports. Obtain copies of all tests. Do research; educate yourself so you are knowledgeable about treatments, risks, natural alternatives, and nutrition.
- Post verses about God's care around your home. Read them often.
- Memorize Isaiah 43:1–2, and review often.
- If confined to home or bed, write and encourage others. Memorize Scripture. Pray for your neighborhood, city, country, and our world. Invite visitors.
- Ask others to pray with you.

RECOMMENDED READING

- *Walking with God through Pain and Suffering.* Tim Keller. Penguin.

- *Health Care Questions Women Ask*. Joe McIlhaney, Jr. Baker.
- *Same Lake, Different Boat: Coming Alongside People Touched by Disability*. Stephanie Huback. P&R.
- *Pain: The Plight of Fallen Man*. James Halla. Timeless Texts.
- *The Problem of Pain*. C. S. Lewis. HarperOne.
- *Suffering and the Heart of God*. Diane Langberg. New Growth.

· Rape ·

The abuse does not define you or have the last word on your identity. Yes, it is part of your story, but not the end of your story.[1]

Lindsey Holcomb

Rape is never the victim's fault.

 Deuteronomy 22:26 But you shall do nothing to the young woman; she has committed no offense punishable by death. For this case is like that of a man attacking and murdering his neighbor. (ESV)

When evil happens, courts and laws may not always be able or willing to provide punishment or justice, but ultimately God will.

2 Thessalonians 1:5–7 This is evidence of the righteous judgment of God, that you may be considered worthy of the kingdom of

God, for which you are also suffering—since indeed God considers it just to repay with affliction those who afflict you, and to grant relief to you who are afflicted as well as to us, when the Lord Jesus is revealed from heaven with his mighty angels. (ESV)

Luke 18:6–8 Then the Lord said, "Learn a lesson from this unjust judge. Even he rendered a just decision in the end. So don't you think God will surely give justice to his chosen people who cry out to him day and night? Will he keep putting them off? I tell you, he will grant justice to them quickly! But when the Son of Man returns, how many will he find on the earth who have faith?" (NLT)

Deuteronomy 32:35 I will take revenge; I will pay them back. In due time their feet will slip. Their day of disaster will arrive, and their destiny will overtake them. (NLT)

Cling to true peace and comfort in Jesus Christ.

1 John 4:4 But you belong to God, my dear children. You have already won a victory over those people, because the Spirit who lives in you is greater than the spirit who lives in the world. (NLT)

Psalm 34:18–19 The LORD is near to the brokenhearted and saves those who are crushed in spirit. Many are the afflictions of the righteous, but the LORD delivers him out of them all. (NASB)

Hebrews 12:1–3 And let us run with perseverance the race marked out for us, fixing our eyes on Jesus, the pioneer and perfecter of faith. For the joy set before him he endured the cross, scorning its shame, and sat down at the right hand of the throne of God. Consider him who endured such opposition from sinners, so that you will not grow weary and lose heart. (NIV)

Isaiah 41:9–10 You whom I took from the ends of the earth, and called from its farthest corners, saying to you, "You are my servant, I have chosen you and not cast you off"; fear not, for I am with you; be not dismayed, for I am your God; I will strengthen you, I will help you, I will uphold you with my righteous right hand. (ESV)

Indeed, God hates all wicked behavior. . . . God does not cause men to rape their sisters, nor does God tempt his human creatures with evil. God's sovereignty must not be understood to mean that God is behind such evil acts and that he is in any sense their cause.[2]

Jerram Barrs

PRACTICAL LIVING

- Medical attention is essential. Rape should be reported to law enforcement.
- Secrets have power and can control us. Seek trusted Christian counsel: a pastor, counselor, friend, and a support group. Don't try to deal with this on your own.
- Seek legal protection if necessary.
- Journal your thoughts, struggles, and feelings. Writing your situation out can be much easier than saying it aloud at times.

RECOMMENDED READING

- *Rid of My Disgrace: Hope and Healing for Victims of Sexual Assault.* Justin Holcomb and Lindsey Holcomb. Crossway.
- *Is It My Fault? Hope and Healing for Those Suffering Domestic Violence.* Lindsey Holcomb. Moody.
- *Sexual Abuse: Beauty for Ashes.* Robert Kellemen. P&R.
- *Walking with God through Pain and Suffering.* Tim Keller. Penguin.

- "Predator, Prey, and Protector: Helping Victims Think and Act from Psalm 10" in *Journal of Biblical Counseling*, vol. 16. David Powlison.
- *Trusting God: Even When Life Hurts*. Jerry Bridges. NavPress.
- *Suffering and the Heart of God*. Diane Langberg. New Growth.

Sexuality

Lust
Marital Sex
Pornography
Sexual Purity

We must pay the most careful attention, therefore,

to what we have heard, so that we do not drift away.

Hebrews 2:1 NIV

· Lust ·

The scary deception of sin is that, at the point of sinning, sin doesn't look all that sinful.[1]

Paul Tripp

Lust is a sinful desire that begins in the mind.

Matthew 5:28 But I say, anyone who even looks at a woman with lust has already committed adultery with her in his heart. (NLT)

1 Peter 2:11 Dear friends, I urge you, as foreigners and exiles, to abstain from sinful desires, which wage war against your soul. (NIV)

Lust is caused by disobedience to God's Word.

 Psalm 119:9, 11 How can a young person stay pure? By obeying your word. . . . I have hidden your word in my heart, that I might not sin against you. (NLT)

Ephesians 4:22 You were taught, with regard to your former way of life, to put off your old self, which is being corrupted by its deceitful desires. (NIV)

Lust is a part of Satan's plan and attack.

1 John 2:16–17 For all that is in the world, the lust of the flesh and the lust of the eyes and the boastful pride of life, is not from the Father, but is from the world. The world is passing away, and also its lusts; but the one who does the will of God lives forever. (NASB)

1 John 5:19 We know that we are from God, and the whole world lies in the power of the evil one. (ESV)

God provides us with the strength to resist lust and live obediently.

Ephesians 6:10–11 Finally, be strong in the Lord and in the strength of his might. Put on the whole armor of God, that you may be able to stand against the schemes of the devil. (ESV)

1 Peter 4:1–2 Therefore, since Christ has suffered in the flesh, arm yourselves also with the same purpose, because he who has suffered in the flesh has ceased from sin, so as to live the rest of the time in the flesh no longer for the lusts of men, but for the will of God. (NASB)

Be on guard; be aware of what causes you to be tempted.

Job 31:1 I made a covenant with my eyes not to look with lust at a young woman. (NLT)

1 Thessalonians 4:3–5 For this is the will of God, your sanctification; that is, that you abstain from sexual immorality; that each of you know how to possess his own vessel in sanctification and honor, not in lustful passion, like the Gentiles who do not know God. (NASB)

. . . .

The God we worship is indeed a God of love. Which does not, according to any verse in the Bible, make sexual sin acceptable. But it does, by witness of a thousand verses all over the Bible, make every one of our sexual sins changeable, redeemable, and wondrously forgivable.[2]

Kevin DeYoung

. . . .

With God's help, it is possible to avoid lustful thoughts.

2 Timothy 2:22 Now flee from youthful lusts and pursue righteousness, faith, love and peace, with those who call on the Lord from a pure heart. (NASB)

Titus 2:12 It teaches us to say "No" to ungodliness and worldly passions, and to live self-controlled, upright and godly lives in this present age. (NIV)

1 Corinthians 10:13 No temptation has overtaken you that is not common to man. God is faithful, and he will not let you be tempted beyond your ability, but with the temptation he will also provide the way of escape, that you may be able to endure it. (ESV)

Romans 6:12–13 Therefore do not let sin reign in your mortal body so that you obey its lusts, and do not go on presenting the members of your body to sin as instruments of unrighteousness; but present yourselves to God as those alive from the dead, and your members as instruments of righteousness to God. (NASB)

PRACTICAL LIVING

- Identify triggers (movies, reading material, music, time of day, places, etc.) and work toward minimizing and eliminating them.
- Listen to Tim Keller's sermon "Love and Lust" (available online at GospelInLife.com).
- Research the meaning of "idol," and locate ten scriptural texts dealing with idolatry.
- Memorize 2 Timothy 2:22 and 1 Corinthians 10:13. Review each day.

- Write out a plan of action to defeat temptation when it comes. Include someone to keep you accountable.
- Print the article "Modesty, Objectivism, and Human Value" by Richard Poupard (available online at Equip.org) and take notes in the margins as you read. Underline concepts you find meaningful and want to remember.
- See related topics: Contentment, Self-Worth, and Sexual Purity.

RECOMMENDED READING

- *Counterfeit Gods*. Tim Keller. Dutton.
- *Finally Free: Fighting for Purity with the Power of Grace*. Heath Lambert. Zondervan.
- *Real Sex: The Naked Truth about Chastity*. Lauren Winner. Brazos.
- *Dirty Girls Come Clean*. Crystal Renaud. Moody.
- *Closing the Window: Steps to Living Porn Free*. Timothy Chester. IVP Books.
- *Intimate Issues*. Linda Dillow and Lorraine Pintus. Water-Brook.
- *Create in Me a Pure Heart*. Steve and Kathy Gallagher. Pure Life Ministries.
- *You Can Change*. Tim Chester. Crossway.

· Marital Sex ·

Hundreds of variables shape how we see sex within marriage: the way we were raised, the churches we go to, boyfriends we dated, circumstances beyond our control, past relationships, people who have wounded us, our spouses—so many things shape our feelings about sex, for good or for ill. Sex, even in marriage, can cause pain and heartache. But the Bible says a healthy sex life in marriage is worth pursuing.

. . . .

Without joyful, loving sex, the friction in a marriage will bring about anger, resentment, hardness, and disappointment. Rather than being the commitment that holds you together, it can become a force to divide you. Never give up working on your sex life.[1]

Tim Keller

. . . .

God created sex, and sexual intimacy in marriage is part of his design.

Genesis 1:27 So God created man in his own image, in the image of God he created him; male and female he created them. (ESV)

Genesis 2:24–25 For this reason a man shall leave his father and his mother, and be joined to his wife; and they shall become one flesh. And the man and his wife were both naked and were not ashamed. (NASB)

. . . .

The gigantic secret of the joy of sex is this: Sex is good because the God who created sex is good. . . . God is glorified greatly when we receive his gift with thanksgiving and enjoy it the way he meant for it to be enjoyed. The reason we like sex so much is that it is a little bit like the God who created it.²

Ben Patterson

. . . .

God created sex for practical purposes, but also as a gift for joy and pleasure.

Isaiah 62:5 As the bridegroom rejoices over the bride, so shall your God rejoice over you. (ESV)

Song of Solomon 1:2 Let him kiss me with the kisses of his mouth! For your love is better than wine. (ESV)

Song of Solomon 4:9–11 My bride: you have captivated my heart with one glance of your eyes, with one jewel of your neck-lace. How beautiful is your love. . . . How much better is your love than wine, and the fragrance of your oils than any spice! Your lips drip nectar, my bride; honey and milk are under your tongue; the fragrance of your garments is like the fragrance of Lebanon. (ESV)

Proverbs 5:18–19 May your fountain be blessed, and may you rejoice in the wife of your youth. A loving doe, a graceful deer— may her breasts satisfy you always, may you ever be intoxicated with her love. (NIV)

All good things point to the Creator.

James 1:17 Every good gift and every perfect gift is from above, coming down from the Father of lights with whom there is no variation or shadow due to change. (ESV)

Christians don't set parameters around sexuality because it is dirty, but rather because it is so good—it is special and unique.[3]

Nathan Miller

The husband is responsible to satisfy his wife sexually, and the wife to satisfy her husband.

 1 Corinthians 7:3–4 The husband should give to his wife her conjugal rights, and likewise the wife to her husband. For the wife does not have authority over her own body, but the husband does. Likewise the husband does not have authority over his own body, but the wife does. (ESV)

Sex within marriage is commanded.

1 Corinthians 7:5 Do not deprive one another, except perhaps by agreement for a limited time, that you may devote yourselves to prayer; but then come together again, so that Satan may not tempt you because of your lack of self-control. (ESV)

God designed sexual relations for married couples only.

Proverbs 5:15–17 Drink water from your own cistern, running water from your own well. Should your springs overflow in the streets, your streams of water in the public squares? Let them be yours alone, never to be shared with strangers. (NIV)

Hebrews 13:4 Let marriage be held in honor among all, and let the marriage bed be undefiled, for God will judge the sexually immoral and adulterous. (ESV)

While intimacy should be a constant in the marriage, there will be times where illness or personal crisis makes having sex inadvisable. Sex is never to be demanded.

1 Corinthians 13:4–7 Love is patient and kind; love does not envy or boast; it is not arrogant or rude. It does not insist on its own way; it is not irritable or resentful; it does not rejoice at wrongdoing, but rejoices with the truth. Love bears all things, believes all things, hopes all things, endures all things. (ESV)

Philippians 2:3–4 Do nothing from selfishness or empty conceit, but with humility of mind regard one another as more important than yourselves; do not merely look out for your own personal interests, but also for the interests of others. (NASB)

PRACTICAL LIVING

- Listen to Tim Keller's series "Sex, Singleness, and Marriage" together (available online at GospelInLife.com).
- Each spouse needs to communicate freely what is pleasing to them. Enjoy what is mutually pleasurable.
- Plan times away from home as a couple—date nights, weekends away, etc.
- For physical problems or pain, see a physician.
- Sexual intimacy is a barometer within marriage. Be sure to practice good communication, forgiveness, conflict resolution, and dealing with issues raising children.
- Understand that intimacy is a part of God's design; he can help us make this a strong part of our marriages.
- See related topics: Forgiving Others, Sexual Purity, Contentment, Disappointment, Adultery, and Guilt.

RECOMMENDED READING

- *The Meaning of Marriage.* Tim and Kathy Keller. Penguin.
- "The Gospel and Sex." Tim Keller. (Available online at Gospel InLife.com.)
- *Intimate Issues.* Linda Dillow. WaterBrook.
- *Intended for Pleasure.* Ed Wheat. Zondervan.
- *The Gift of Sex.* Clifford Penner. Thomas Nelson.
- *Sheet Music.* Kevin Leman. Tyndale.
- *A Biblical Guide to Love, Sex, and Marriage.* Derek and Rosemary Thomas. Evangelical Press.

· Pornography ·

Pornography is one of the most pervasive and dangerous issues our society faces today. It's easily accessed through our phones, computers, and with the rise of popular erotic books, even through our e-readers and libraries. Tim Challies observes, "Erotica has evolved. It has moved from shop-floor to shop-front, from might-read to must-read, from late-night theater to prime-time theater."[1]

Pornography negatively affects our brains, hearts, how we interact with one another, and our society as a whole.[2] But we know the good news: the gospel and forgiveness through Christ change and renew everything. We don't need to be slaves to our addictions, because Christ has overcome the world and can renew our minds. As Paul writes, "Do not conform to the pattern of this world, but be transformed by the renewing of your mind. Then you will be able to test and approve what God's will is—his good, pleasing and perfect will" (Romans 12:2 NIV).

Our eyes must be protected from viewing ungodliness.

 Psalm 101:3–4 I will not look with approval on anything that is vile. I hate what faithless people do; I will have no part in it. The perverse of heart shall be far from me; I will have nothing to do with what is evil. (NIV)

Matthew 5:28 But I say to you that everyone who looks at a woman with lust for her has already committed adultery with her in his heart. (NASB)

Isaiah 1:16 Wash yourselves, make yourselves clean; remove the evil of your deeds from My sight. Cease to do evil. (NASB)

Few secular commentators dare to say what many of us see: our porn problem is a moral problem, with drastic consequences.[3]

Halee Gray Scott

Guard your hearts and your minds.

Philippians 4:8 Finally, brothers and sisters, whatever is true, whatever is noble, whatever is right, whatever is pure, whatever is lovely, whatever is admirable—if anything is excellent or praiseworthy—think about such things. (NIV)

Philippians 4:6–7 Do not be anxious about anything, but in every situation, by prayer and petition, with thanksgiving, present your requests to God. And the peace of God, which transcends all understanding, will guard your hearts and your minds in Christ Jesus. (NIV)

Pornography affects every aspect of a person's life.

Luke 11:34–36 Your eye is the lamp of your body. When your eye is healthy, your whole body is full of light, but when it is bad, your body is full of darkness. Therefore be careful lest the light in you be darkness. If then your whole body is full of light, having no part dark, it will be wholly bright, as when a lamp with its rays gives you light. (ESV)

James 1:14–15 But each person is tempted when he is lured and enticed by his own desire. Then desire when it has conceived gives birth to sin, and sin when it is fully grown brings forth death. (ESV)

. . . .

Americans are more tolerant of porn use than ever—even while research is confirming that it's worse than we thought.[4]

Halee Gray Scott

. . . .

Jesus has already conquered the world on our behalf.

1 John 5:3–5 In fact, this is love for God: to keep his commands. And his commands are not burdensome, for everyone born of God overcomes the world. This is the victory that has overcome the world, even our faith. Who is it that overcomes the world? Only the one who believes that Jesus is the Son of God. (NIV)

John 16:33 I have told you these things, so that in me you may have peace. In this world you will have trouble. But take heart! I have overcome the world. (NIV)

1 John 4:4 You, dear children, are from God and have overcome them, because the one who is in you is greater than the one who is in the world. (NIV)

There is hope. Freedom from this sin is possible.

Romans 6:12–14 Let not sin therefore reign in your mortal bodies, to make you obey its passions. Do not present your members to sin as instruments for unrighteousness, but present yourselves to God as those who have been brought from death to life, and your members to God as instruments for righteousness. For sin will have no dominion over you, since you are not under law but under grace. (ESV)

2 Corinthians 5:17 Therefore, if anyone is in Christ, he is a new creation. The old has passed away; behold, the new has come. (ESV)

Nothing is hidden from the eyes of God.

Psalm 90:8 You have set our iniquities before you, our secret sins in the light of your presence. (ESV)

Proverbs 15:3 The eyes of the LORD are in every place, keeping watch on the evil and the good. (ESV)

You must remove pornography from your life.

Psalm 119:37 Turn my eyes from worthless things, and give me life through your word. (NLT)

Psalm 32:3–5 When I kept silent about my sin, my body wasted away through my groaning all day long. For day and night Your hand was heavy upon me; my vitality was drained away as with the fever heat of summer. I acknowledged my sin to You, and my iniquity I did not hide; I said, "I will confess my transgressions to the LORD"; and You forgave the guilt of my sin. (NASB)

Job 31:1 I made a covenant with my eyes not to look with lust at a young woman. (NLT)

Romans 13:14 Instead, clothe yourself with the presence of the Lord Jesus Christ. And don't let yourself think about ways to indulge your evil desires. (NLT)

Seek accountability with those who experience freedom from this sin.

2 Timothy 2:21–22 Therefore, if anyone cleanses himself from what is dishonorable, he will be a vessel for honorable use, set apart as holy . . . ready for every good work. So flee youthful passions and pursue righteousness, faith, love, and peace, along with those who call on the Lord from a pure heart. (ESV)

Galatians 6:1–2 Dear brothers and sisters, if another believer is overcome by some sin, you who are godly should gently and humbly help that person back onto the right path. And be careful not to fall into the same temptation yourself. Share each other's burdens, and in this way obey the law of Christ. (NLT)

 Romans 12:2 Don't become so well-adjusted to your culture that you fit into it without even thinking. Instead, fix your attention on God. You'll be changed from the inside out. Readily recognize what he wants from you, and quickly respond to it. Unlike the culture around you, always dragging you down to its level of immaturity, God brings the best out of you, develops well-formed maturity in you. (MSG)

PRACTICAL LIVING

- Take protective action for your family. Start with Tim Challies's helpful step-by-step guide: "The Porn-Free Family Plan" (available online at Challies.com).
- Write on a card: "I have two choices—obeying God or obeying self. Who will I honor?"

- Read Tim Challies's article: "7 Good Reasons to Stop Looking at Porn Right Now" (available online at Challies.com).
- Use the resources available at the website Fight the New Drug (www.fightthenewdrug.com), which explains how pornography affects our brains, our hearts, and our world.
- Rid your living space of items that lead to temptation (books, photos, etc.). Do not go to places where temptation grows. Place safeguards on your computer, your phones, and other electronic devices.
- Seek accountability.
- To reprogram your mind away from sinful viewing and towards pure thinking, make a list comparing and contrasting the hurt and destruction of pornography with the life and freedom that comes with purity.
- See related topics: Lust, Sexual Purity, and Addiction.

RECOMMENDED READING

- *Closing the Window: Steps to Living Porn Free*. Tim Chester. IVP Books.
- *Finally Free: Fighting for Purity with the Power of Grace*. Heath Lambert. Zondervan.
- *Sexual Sanity for Women: Healing from Sexual and Relational Brokenness*. Ellen Dykas (editor). Harvest USA.
- *Eyes of Integrity*. Craig Gross and Jason Harper. Baker.
- *Pornography: Slaying the Dragon*. David Powlison. P&R.
- *Undefiled: Redemption From Sexual Sin, Restoration For Broken Relationships*. Harry Schaumburg. Moody.
- *Captured by a Better Vision*. Tim Chester. IVP Books.
- *Dirty Girls Come Clean*. Crystal Renaud. Moody.

- "My Husband Is into Pornography. What Should I Do?" in *Intimate Issues*. Linda Dillow. WaterBrook.
- *When His Secret Sin Breaks Your Heart*. Kathy Gallagher. Pure Life Ministries.

· Sexual Purity ·

How we handle our sexual life can either affirm or contradict what we believe about God. God gave himself to us unconditionally in Christ, and he calls us to give ourselves unconditionally to him. God does not offer or ask for intimacy without complete whole-life commitment. If you demand intimacy yet keep control of your life, you are a living contradiction of both the way God relates to you and the way we are to relate to each other in the Christian community.[1]

Tim Keller

God made our bodies and our desires.

Genesis 1:27 So God created man in his own image, in the image of God he created him; male and female he created them. (ESV)

1 Corinthians 6:19–20 Or do you not know that your body is a temple of the Holy Spirit who is in you, whom you have from God, and that you are not your own? For you have been bought with a price: therefore glorify God in your body. (NASB)

Sex is meant to be a signpost of God's great love for us.

James 1:17 Every good gift and every perfect gift is from above, coming down from the Father of lights, with whom there is no variation or shadow due to change. (ESV)

Ephesians 5:31–32 "For this reason a man will leave his father and mother and be united to his wife, and the two will become one flesh." This is a profound mystery—but I am talking about Christ and the church. (NIV)

God made sex for marriage.

Genesis 2:24–25 Therefore a man leaves his father and mother and embraces his wife. They become one flesh. The two of them, the Man and his Wife, were naked, but they felt no shame. (MSG)

Hebrews 13:4 Let marriage be held in honor among all, and let the marriage bed be undefiled, for God will judge the sexually immoral and adulterous. (ESV)

God made sex, and it's the most precious things that need the most protecting.

Song of Solomon 4:9–11 My bride: you have captivated my heart with one glance of your eyes, with one jewel of your necklace. How beautiful is your love. . . . How much better is your love than wine, and the fragrance of your oils than any spice! Your lips drip nectar, my bride; honey and milk are under your tongue; the fragrance of your garments is like the fragrance of Lebanon. (ESV)

Proverbs 5:18–19 May your fountain be blessed, and may you rejoice in the wife of your youth. A loving doe, a graceful deer— may her breasts satisfy you always, may you ever be intoxicated with her love. (NIV)

Don't unite with someone physically unless you are also willing to unite with the person emotionally, personally, socially, economically, and legally. Don't become physically naked and vulnerable to the other person without becoming vulnerable in every other way.[2]

Tim and Kathy Keller

Saving sex for marriage isn't about God keeping something pleasurable from you; it's about what God wants for you.

Romans 7:4–6 So, my brothers and sisters, you also died to the law through the body of Christ, that you might belong to another, to him who was raised from the dead, in order that we might bear fruit for God. For when we were in the realm of the flesh, the sinful passions aroused by the law were at work in us, so that we bore fruit for death. But now, by dying to what once bound us, we have been released from the law so that we serve in the new way of the Spirit, and not in the old way of the written code. (NIV)

Protecting purity in marriage begins long before marriage.

Psalm 119:9–11 How can a young person stay on the path of purity? By living according to your word. I seek you with all my heart; do not let me stray from your commands. I have hidden your word in my heart that I might not sin against you. (NIV)

Sex is God's appointed way for two people to reciprocally say to one another, "I belong completely, permanently, and exclusively to you." You must not use sex to say anything less.[3]

Tim and Kathy Keller

Sexual immorality is sin and must be avoided.

Romans 13:14 Instead, clothe yourself with the presence of the Lord Jesus Christ. And don't let yourself think about ways to indulge your evil desires. (NLT)

James 1:21 Therefore, get rid of all moral filth and the evil that is so prevalent and humbly accept the word planted in you, which can save you. (NIV)

1 Thessalonians 4:3–6 It is God's will that you should be sanctified: that you should avoid sexual immorality; that each of you should learn to control your own body in a way that is holy and honorable, not in passionate lust like the pagans, who do not know God; and that in this matter no one should wrong or take advantage of a brother or sister. The Lord will punish all those who commit such sins, as we told you and warned you before. (NIV)

Purity is commanded by God.

1 Peter 1:15–16 But as He who called you is holy, you also be holy in all your conduct, because it is written, "Be holy, for I am holy." (NKJV)

1 Thessalonians 4:7 For God did not call us to be impure, but to live a holy life. (NIV)

Pursue what is pure; living purely is more than just avoiding premarital sex.

 2 Timothy 2:22 Run from anything that stimulates youthful lusts. Instead, pursue righteous living, faithfulness, love, and peace. Enjoy the companionship of those who call on the Lord with pure hearts. (NLT)

Romans 8:5–6 For those who live according to the flesh set their minds on the things of the flesh, but those who live according to

the Spirit set their minds on the things of the Spirit. For to set the mind on the flesh is death, but to set the mind on the Spirit is life and peace. (ESV)

Purity is more than just avoiding sexual intercourse. Purity starts in the mind.

Job 31:1 I made a covenant with my eyes not to look lustfully at a young woman. (NIV)

Matthew 5:28 But I say to you that everyone who looks at a woman with lustful intent has already committed adultery with her in his heart. (ESV)

Determine to be obedient with God's help.

Isaiah 50:7 Because the Sovereign LORD helps me, I will not be disgraced. Therefore, I have set my face like a stone, determined to do his will. And I know that I will not be put to shame. (NLT)

Ephesians 6:10–13 Finally, be strong in the Lord and in his mighty power. Put on the full armor of God so that you can take your stand against the devil's schemes. For our struggle is not against flesh and blood, but against the rulers, against the authorities, against the powers of this dark world and against the spiritual forces of evil in the heavenly realms. Therefore put on the full armor of God, so that when the day of evil comes, you may be able to stand your ground, and after you have done everything, to stand. (NIV)

PRACTICAL LIVING

- Listen to Tim Keller's sermon "Love and Lust" and his series "Sex, Singleness, and Marriage" (available online at Gospel InLife.com).

253

- Read Tim Keller's essay "The Gospel and Sex" (available online at GospelInLife.com). How does the gospel change your views about purity and sexuality?
- Instead of spending time alone with the opposite sex, build relationships in group situations with family and friends.
- Make it your focus and ultimate goal to please and obey God. Avoid the person who pressures you to compromise. See 2 Corinthians 5:9.
- When in a relationship, have good accountability. Have people in your life who will ask tough questions and speak truth into your relationships.
- Think about boundaries before you get into a situation where you are tempted. Many dating couples have found this helpful, as they think about their physical relationship and seek to live purely: if you can't do it in a public place, it's probably safe to say you shouldn't be doing it in private.
- See related topics: Singleness, Marriage, Lust, Sin and God's Forgiveness, and Guilt.

RECOMMENDED READING

- "The Gospel and Sex." Tim Keller. (Available online at Gospel InLife.com.)
- *Pure Heart: A Woman's Guide to Sexual Integrity.* Shellie R. Warren. Baker.
- *Sexual Sanity for Women: Healing from Sexual and Relational Brokenness.* Ellen Dykas (editor). New Growth Press.
- *The Meaning of Marriage.* Tim and Kathy Keller. Penguin.
- "Sex and the Single Woman." Fabienne Harford. (Available online at TheGospelCoalition.org.)

Appendices

We have this hope as an anchor

for the soul, firm and secure.

Hebrews 6:19 NIV

Appendix A

Characteristics of God

God Is . . .

Eternal *Exod. 3:14; Ps. 102:12; Heb. 13:8*

Faithful *Ps. 89:1–8; Lam. 3:22–23; 1 Cor. 1:9*

Good *Exod. 34:6–7; Ps. 25:8; James 1:17*

Gracious *Ps. 145:17; Rom. 1:5; Rom. 3:24*

Holy *Exod. 3:5–6; Ps. 99:2–3; Rev. 4:8*

Immutable *Ps. 102:25–28; Mal. 3:6; James 1:17*

Infinite *Deut. 33:27; Ps. 147:5; Rom. 11:33*

Just *Exod. 34:6–7; Ps. 99:4; 1 Pet. 1:17*

Light *Isa. 60:19; James 1:17; 1 John 1:5*

Love *Deut. 7:7–8; Rom. 8:35, 39; 1 John 4:8, 16*

Merciful *Ps. 6:4; Eph. 2:4; Titus 3:5; 1 Pet. 1:3*

Omnipotent—All-powerful *Jer. 32:17; Rom. 11:36; Eph. 1:11*

Omnipresent—Present everywhere *Job 11:7–9; Ps. 90:1–2; 139:7–10*

Omniscient—All-knowing *Ps. 147:5; Acts 15:18; Heb. 4:13*

Patient *Ps. 103:8; Rom. 15:5; 1 Pet. 3:20*

Perfect *Deut. 32:4; Ps. 92:15; Matt. 5:48*

Righteous *Ps. 145:17; Jer. 9:24; 1 John 2:29*
Self-Existing *Exod. 3:14; Ps. 90:2; Col. 1:15–17*
Sovereign *Ps. 115:3; Matt. 10:29; 1 Pet. 3:17*
Trustworthy/Reliable *Num. 23:19; Ps. 102:26–27; Mal. 3:6*
Truth *John 14:6; 16:13; 1 John 5:20*
Wise *Prov. 3:19–20; Rom. 16:27; 1 Tim. 1:17*

Compiled by Elizabeth Clevenger, Calvary University

Appendix B

Bible Reading Plans

The Bible Project
https://thebibleproject.com/reading-plan/

Bible Gateway (five different plans)
http://www.biblegateway.com/reading-plans/

One Year Plan (three daily readings)
http://www.arcamax.com/ttb-yr.html

United Methodist Church (straight through, one year)
http://www.ngumc.org/readthebibleinayear

TheBible.net (straight through, one year)
http://www.thebible.net/read/sched.html

Appendix C

Names of God

Abba (Father) *Exod. 4:22–23; Num. 1:9; 1 Sam. 16:6; Ps. 2:7; Isa. 63:8, 16; Mal. 1:6; Rom. 8:15; Gal. 4:6*

El Elyon (The Most High) *Gen. 14:18; Ps. 38:2*

El Gibhor (The Mighty God) *Isa. 9:6*

El HaNe'eman (The Faithful God) *Deut. 7:9*

Elohim Mauzi (God of My Strength) *Ps. 43:2*

Elohim Mikarov (God Who Is Near) *Jer. 23:23*

Elohim Mishpat (The God of Justice) *Isa. 30:18*

Elohim Selichot (God of Forgiveness) *Neh. 9:17*

Elohim Tehilati (God of My Praise) *Ps. 109:1*

El Olam (Everlasting) *Gen. 21:33; Ps. 10:16*

El Roi (The God Who Sees) *Gen. 16:7–16*

El Shaddai (The Almighty) *Gen. 17:1*

El Yeshuati (God of My Salvation) *Isa. 12:2*

Immanu El (God Is with Us) *Isa. 7:14*

Jehovah Ganan (Lord Our Defense) *Ps. 89:18*

Jehovah-Jireh (The Lord Will Provide) *Gen. 22:14; 1 John 4:9; Phil. 4:19*

Jehovah Rapha (Lord That Heals) *Isa. 53:4–5*

Jehovah Sabaoth (The Lord of Hosts) *1 Sam. 1:3*

Jehovah Shalom (The Lord Is Peace) *Jude 6:24; Isa. 9:6; Rom. 8:31–35*

Jehovah Tsidkenu (Lord Our Righteousness) *Jer. 33:16; 1 Cor. 1:30*

Compiled by Elizabeth Clevenger, Calvary University

Appendix D

Decision Making

When you're faced with a decision, here are some questions you can ask yourself to determine if the voice you hear is God speaking to you:

- Is it consistent with Scripture?
- Is it consistent with the character of God?
- Does it lead to change or growth in your life?
- Does it lead to the restoration of relationships?
- Is there a sense of healing and a release from past sin or pain?
- Is there a sense of peace, a lessening of anxiety, a feeling of contentment where once there was striving?
- Does it lead to conviction instead of guilt?

We sometimes mistake Satan's voice for God's, because Satan's voice fits so well with our own distortions and misunderstandings about God and how we think he feels about us. But God speaks to us in a way that is completely different from the condemnation of Satan.

How can you tell the difference? Satan communicates in the following way:

- **Tone:** Accusing, nagging, and mocking, generates fear and causes confusion.

- **Vague:** Generates an overall sense of guilt, as if everything is wrong. Creates feelings of hopelessness and weakness.
- **Discourages:** Attacks your self-confidence. Tells you that you are weak and worthless.
- **Brings up the past:** Replays your sin and shame. Reminds you of your poor choices.
- **Rejects:** Produces the feeling that God has rejected you as unworthy and unholy. Portrays God as judge and you as a miserable sinner.
- **Isolates:** Gives suggestions that cause you to withdraw from others.
- **Negative:** Tells you that the horrible way you feel is the way it is.

The conviction of the Holy Spirit is just the opposite:

- **Tone:** Gentle, loving, imploring, and urges your return to God.
- **Specific:** Tells you to take a specific action in response to sin; freedom follows.
- **Encourages:** Says you can rely on God's power, not your strength.
- **Releases you from the past:** Tells you your sins are forgiven, never to be held against you.
- **Attracts:** Generates an expectation of kindness, love, and a new beginning with God's help.
- **Draws into fellowship:** Sends others to minister to you in love, as well as sends you to others. Speaks of God's unchanging nature and steadfast love.
- **Truthful:** States the facts about you and God.

Taken from *Come To Me* © 2002 by Elaine Hamilton and Kathy Escobar. Used by permission of Discovery House. Grand Rapids, MI. All rights reserved.

Appendix E

What Does God Do with Forgiven Sin?

Confess—Repent—Forgiven

After confession and repentance, God forgives. At that point, how does he see our sin?

Sins are as far as the east is from the west he removes transgressions—Psalm 103:12

Sins shall be as white as snow—Isaiah 1:18

He puts sins behind his back—Isaiah 38:17

He remembers the sins no more—Hebrews 8:12

He casts sins into the depths of the sea—Micah 7:18–20

He treads iniquities underfoot—Micah 7:19

He does not retain his anger—Micah 7:18

He forgives the guilt of sin—Psalm 32:5

He sets the believer free, there is no condemnation—Romans 8:1–2

He does not keep a record of sins—Psalm 130:3–4

He sweeps offenses away like a cloud, like the morning mist—Isaiah 44:22

He will freely pardon—Isaiah 55:7

He rescues—Colossians 1:13

He turns a person into a new creation, taking old and bringing new—2 Corinthians 5:17

He purifies from all unrighteousness—1 John 1:9

He covers the sin—Psalm 32:1

He refreshes with his presence—Acts 3:19

He restores—Jeremiah 29:11–14

Appendix F

Applying the Gospel to Daily Life for Those Abused

1. **God's Mission Statement:** *"I Am Indispensable"*

   In what specific ways can your life communicate your belief in and surrender to God's mission statement?

2. **The Damage of Loss or Trust: The Attempted Destruction of Faith**

   How has your openness to trust in God and connection with others been impacted by the abuse you suffered? How does your response to your abuse contrast and compare with Tamar's response in 2 Samuel 13:1–12?

3. **The Damage of Powerlessness: The Attempted Destruction of Hope**

   How has your ability to dream, hope, long, want, and choose been affected by the abuse you suffered? How does your response to your abuse contrast and compare with Tamar's response in 2 Samuel 13:2, 11–14?

4. The Damage of Shame: The Attempted Destruction of Peace

In response to your abuse, in what ways have you struggled with shame, self-contempt, feelings of rejection and disgrace, guilt, and difficulties connecting deeply? How does your response to your abuse contrast and compare with Tamar's response in 2 Samuel 13:13–17?

5. The Damage of Being Used and Feeling Useless: The Attempted Destruction of Love

In response to your abuse, in what ways have you struggled with feelings of worthlessness and lovelessness? How does your response to your abuse contrast and compare with Tamar's response in 2 Samuel 13:14–20?

6. Sustaining Faith: Preserving Trust

Who has truly entered the battle for your soul—entered the black hole with you? How has their presence impacted you? In what ways are you embracing God again and experiencing the embrace of God?

7. Healing Hope: Clinging to the Goodness of God

In what ways are you beginning to see God weave good out of the evil of your abuse? In your weakness, how are you finding and relying upon God's strength? How are you finding God?

8. Reconciling Peace: Receiving Christ's Grace

Through Christ, how have you been overwhelming sin with grace by taking sin seriously? By taking the sinful abuse seriously? By defeating the lie of "false guilt"? By exploring possible sinful responses to the sinful abuse?

9. Guiding Love: Offering Beauty for Ashes

What does renewed and empowered faith and trust look like for you? Renewed and empowered hope and joy? Renewed and empowered peace and shalom? Renewed and empowered love and meaningful service?

10. Grace: Prescription for Our Disgrace

Through Christ's grace, how will you continue to journey down life's path with God's prescription for your disgrace—grace? Through grace, how will your life be God's masterpiece displaying the splendor of Christ's grace?

Taken from *Sexual Abuse* by Robert Kellemen. Used with permission from P&R Publishing Co. P.O. Box 817, Phillipsburg, NJ. www.prpbooks.com

Notes

Introduction

1. Philip Yancey, *The Jesus I Never Knew* (Grand Rapids: Zondervan, 1995), 85.
2. Ibid., 23.
3. Dorothy L. Sayers, *Are Women Human? Penetrating, Sensible, and Witty Essays on the Role of Women in Society* (Grand Rapids: Eerdmans, 2005), 68.

The Good News

1. David Martyn Lloyd-Jones, quoted in Timothy Keller, "Gospel-Centered Ministry," Gospel Coalition Conference, 2007. Posted January 31, 2014, on Key Life, "Good News vs. Good Advice," http://www.keylife.org/articles/good-news -vs-good-advice.
2. Timothy and Kathy Keller, *The Meaning of Marriage*, reprint ed. (New York: Penguin, 2013), 40.

Who Is God?

1. C. S. Lewis, *Mere Christianity* (New York: HarperOne, 2000), 177.
2. John Piper, *The Pleasures of God*, rev. ed. (Portland: Multnomah, 2000), 11–12.
3. Timothy Keller and Sam Shammas, "New City Catechism," Redeemer Presbyterian Church, accessed February 27, 2017, at http://www.newcitycatechism .com/New_City_Catechism.pdf.

How to Know God

1. David Mathis, *Habits of Grace* (Wheaton: Crossway, 2016).
2. Ibid., 25.

Why the Bible?

1. Sally Lloyd-Jones, *The Jesus Storybook Bible* (Grand Rapids: ZonderKidz, 2007), 14–17.

What to Do with Doubt

1. Alister E. McGrath, *Doubting* (Leicester: IVP, 2006), 13–14; reprint of *Doubt* (1990).
2. Frederick Buechner, *Beyond Words* (New York: HarperOne, 2004), 85.

Sin and God's Forgiveness

1. John Piper, "What Is Sin? The Essence and Root of All Sinning," Desiring God 2015 Conference for Pastors, February 2, 2015, 45:42, http://www.desiring god.org/messages/the-origin-essence-and-definition-of-sin.

Comfort

1. Paul David Tripp, Twitter post, June 11, 2016, accessed August 23, 2016, http://twitter.com/paultripp/status/741618599597592576.

Contentment

1. Shauna Niequist, "Enough," blog entry, January 12, 2011, http://www .shaunaniequist.com/enough/.
2. John Piper, *Future Grace: The Purifying Power of the Promises of God*, rev. ed. (Colorado Springs: Multnomah, 2012), 224.

Hope

1. Paul David Tripp, "Hope in This Broken-Down World," Ligonier Ministries, December 1, 2011, http://www.ligonier.org/learn/articles/hope-in-this-broken -down-world/.
2. Timothy Keller, "Born into Hope" (sermon), 39:23, Redeemer Presbyterian Church, February 4, 2001, http://www.gospelinlife.com/born-into-hope-5221.

Rest

1. Michael Yaconelli, *Messy Spirituality* (Grand Rapids: Zondervan, 2002), 98.
2. Bill Gorman, "Responding to the King: Find Your Rest" (sermon), 35:11, Brookside Campus of Christ Community Evangelical Free Church, May 8, 2016, http://christcommunitykc.org/sermons/.
3. Yaconelli, *Messy Spirituality*, 96.
4. Mark A. Buchanan, *The Rest of God: Restoring Your Soul by Restoring Sabbath* (Nashville: Thomas Nelson, 2006), 93.
5. Bill Gorman, "Responding to the King: Find Your Rest."

Self-Worth

1. Timothy Keller, *The Reason for God*, reprint ed. (New York: Penguin, 2009), 181.

Trials

1. Timothy Keller, *Walking with God through Pain and Suffering* (New York: Penguin, 2015): 58, 180–181.
2. Annie Johnson Flint, "He Giveth More Grace," accessed February 27, 2017, http://library.timelesstruths.org/music/He-Giveth-More-Grace/.

Trust

1. A. W. Tozer, *Knowledge of the Holy*, gift ed. (San Francisco: HarperOne, 1992), 98–99.

Clothing

1. We are indebted to Kevin DeYoung for his thoughtfulness in this area and his article "The Lost Virtue of Modesty," The Gospel Coalition, October 2, 2014, http://blogs.thegospelcoalition.org/kevindeyoung/2014/10/02/the-biblical-virtue-of-modesty/.
2. Ibid.
3. Carolyn Mahaney and Nicole Whitacre, *True Beauty* (Wheaton: Crossway, 2014), 74.
4. Elyse Fitzpatrick, "Gentle Jesus, Meek and . . . Modest," The Gospel Coalition, July 15, 2010, https://www.thegospelcoalition.org/article/gentle-jesus-meek-and-modest.
5. DeYoung, "The Lost Virtue of Modesty."

Decision Making

1. Kevin DeYoung, *Just Do Something* (Chicago: Moody, 2009), 61.

Entertainment

1. Steven Garber, "From Ideologies to Art: Why Work Matters," Patheos, June 14, 2013, http://www.patheos.com/blogs/reintegrate/2013/06/14/from-ideologies-to-art-why-work-matters/.
2. Ibid.
3. Mike Cosper, *The Stories We Tell* (Wheaton: Crossway, 2014), 28–29.
4. N. D. Wilson, "The Dark-Tinted, Truth-Filled Reading List Our Kids Need," *Christianity Today* 58, no. 1 (2014): 30.

Money

1. John Maxwell quoted in Dave Ramsey, *The Total Money Makeover* (Nashville: Thomas Nelson, 2013), 59.
2. C. S. Lewis, *Mere Christianity* (New York: Simon & Schuster, 1996), 182.
3. Dave Ramsey, "The Seven Deadly Debt Sins," blog entry, September 30, 2009, http://www.daveramsey.com/articles/print/articleID/the-seven-deadly-debt-sins/.
4. Dave Ramsey, *More Than Enough* (New York: Penguin, 2002), 213.

5. John Wesley, "The Use of Money," Wesley Center Online: The Sermons of John Wesley, accessed February 28, 2017, http://wesley.nnu.edu/john-wesley/the-sermons-of-john-wesley-1872-edition/sermon-50-the-use-of-money/.

Social Media

1. Samuel James, "The Pleasures and Perils of the Online Life," The Gospel Coalition, February 3, 2016, https://www.thegospelcoalition.org/article/the-pleasures-and-perils-of-the-online-life.

2. Ibid.

Time Management

1. Matt Perman, "The Key to Gospel-Driven Productivity," The Gospel Coalition, January 8, 2016, https://www.thegospelcoalition.org/article/the-key-to-gospel-driven-productivity.

2. Annie Dillard, *The Writing Life* (New York: Harper Perennial, 2013), 32.

3. John Piper, *Don't Waste Your Life*, group study ed. (Wheaton: Crossway, 2007), 147.

Work

1. Perman, "The Key to Gospel-Driven Productivity."

2. Dorothy Sayers, *Letters to a Diminished Church* (Nashville: Thomas Nelson, 2004), 140.

3. Ibid., 139–140.

4. Timothy Keller, *Every Good Endeavor,* reprint ed. (New York: Penguin, 2014), 19.

Bitterness

1. Anne Peterson, "How to Deal with Bitterness," Christian Bible Studies, March 15, 2011, http://www.christianitytoday.com/biblestudies/articles/spiritual formation/hardenedheart.html.

Depression

1. Jeff Forrey, "How the Gospel Transforms Our Fears (Part 1)," Biblical Counseling Coalition, November 7, 2016, http://biblicalcounselingcoalition.org/2016/11/07/how-the-gospel-transforms-our-fears-part-1/.

Difficult Memories

1. Paul David Tripp, *New Morning Mercies* (Wheaton: Crossway, 2014), 8.

Disappointment

1. Courtney Reissig, "You Can't Turn Lemons into Lemonade," The Gospel Coalition, December 2, 2013, https://www.thegospelcoalition.org/article/you-cant-turn-lemons-into-lemonade.

2. Ibid.

3. Shauna Niequist, *Cold Tangerines,* special compilation ed. (Grand Rapids: Zondervan, 2010), 234.

Grief

1. Amy Balentine, personal email, October 2016.

2. Keller, *Walking with God through Pain and Suffering*, 181.

Guilt

1. Kevin DeYoung, "Are Christians Meant To Feel Guilty All The Time?" The Gospel Coalition, May 11, 2010, https://blogs.thegospelcoalition.org/kevinde young/2010/05/11/are-christians-meant-to-feel-guilty-all-the-time/.

Loneliness

1. Keller, *Walking with God through Pain and Suffering*, 304.

2. Elisabeth Elliot, *The Path of Loneliness* (Grand Rapids: Revell, 1998), 153.

3. A. W. Tozer, *Man: The Dwelling Place of God* (Harrisburg, PA: Christian Publications, 1966), 172.

Pride

1. Sam Storms, "How Pride Poisons the Soul," Enjoying God (blog), April 9, 2015, http://www.samstorms.com/enjoying-god-blog/post/how-pride-poisons-the-soul.

2. C. S. Lewis, *Mere Christianity*, rev. and amp. edition (New York: Harper-Collins, 2000), 121–124.

3. Storms, "How Pride Poisons the Soul."

4. John R. W. Stott, "Pride, Humility, and God," Im4God newsletter, May 31, 2007, http://www.im4god.org/newsletter/newsletter5-31-07.shtml.

5. Timothy Keller, *The Freedom of Self-Forgetfulness* (London, UK: 10Publishing, 2012), Kindle edition, location 281 of 431.

Worry

1. Jeff Forrey, "4 Pastoral Truths for Those Scared by the News," Care Leader, June 23, 2016, http://www.careleader.org/4-truths-help-people-frightened-news/.

2. Jerry Bridges, *Respectable Sins* (Leicester, UK: Inter-Varsity, 2007), 65.

Church

1. Tim Keller, "The Difficulty of Community," blog entry, October 1, 2008, http://www.timothykeller.com/blog/2008/10/1/the-difficulty-of-community.

2. Ibid.

3. Matt Perman, "Bill Hybels—The Local Church Is the Hope of the World," What's Best Next (blog), August 10, 2012, https://www.whatsbestnext.com/2012/08/bill-hybels-the-local-church-is-the-hope-of-the-world/.

4. Usually attributed to Abigail VanBuren.

Communication

1. Paul David Tripp, *War of Words* (Phillipsburg, N.J.: P & R, 2000), 15.
2. Nancy Leigh DeMoss, *Lies Women Believe and the Truth That Sets Them Free* (Chicago: Moody, 2001), 33.

Forgiving Others

1. Ken Sande, *The Peacemaker* (Grand Rapids: Baker, 2004), 206–207.
2. C. S. Lewis, "On Forgiveness," *The Weight of Glory* (New York: Harper-Collins, 2001), 181–183.
3. Corrie Ten Boom and Jamie Buckingham, *Tramp for the Lord* (Old Tappan, NJ: Revell, 1974), 57.

Friendship

1. Shauna Niequist, *Cold Tangerines,* special compilation ed. (Grand Rapids: Zondervan, 2010), 50.
2. Tripp, *New Morning Mercies*, 14.
3. C. S. Lewis, *The Four Loves* (New York: Harvest/Harcourt, Brace, & Co., 1991), 78.

Hospitality

1. Dorothy Day, *The Long Loneliness* (New York: Harper and Brothers, 1952), 285.
2. Shauna Niequist, *Bread and Wine* (Grand Rapids: Zondervan, 2013), 250.
3. Eugene H. Peterson, *Christ Plays in Ten Thousand Places* (Grand Rapids: Eerdmans, 2005), 217.
4. Niequist, *Bread and Wine*, 114–115.
5. Ibid., 41.

Marriage

1. Timothy Keller, "The Gospel and Sex," Gospel in Life, April 27, 2010, http://www.gospelinlife.com/the-gospel-and-sex.
2. Ibid.
3. Kathy Keller, *Jesus, Justice, and Gender Roles* (New York: HarperCollins, 2012), Kindle edition, location 456.

Mothering

1. Elizabeth Hawn, personal letter, October 2016.
2. Jen Wilkin, "On Empty Nests, Christian Mommy Guilt, and Misplaced Identity," The Gospel Coalition, August 29, 2016, https://www.thegospelcoalition.org/article/empty-nests-christian-mommy-guilt-misplaced-identity.
3. Ibid.
4. Ibid.

5. We are indebted to Jen Wilkin for this concept and her wise thoughts in this area.

6. Jen Wilkin, "Our Children, Our Neighbors," The Beginning of Wisdom (blog), March 19, 2014, http://jenwilkin.blogspot.com/2014/03/our-children-our-neighbors.html.

7. Ibid.

Singleness

1. Keller, "The Gospel and Sex."

2. Ibid.

Abortion

1. Kevin DeYoung, "Answering the Abortion Question That Is Sure to Come," The Gospel Coalition, January 14, 2016, https://blogs.thegospelcoalition.org/kevindeyoung/2016/01/14/answering-the-abortion-question-that-is-sure-to-come/.

2. Ibid.

Abortion Recovery

1. Marian Jordan Ellis, "Healing After Abortion," Redeemed Girl Ministries, September 10, 2015, http://www.redeemedgirl.org/healing-after-abortion.

2. Ibid.

Addiction

1. Timothy Keller, *Counterfeit Gods: The Empty Promises of Money, Sex, and Power, and the Only Hope That Matters* (New York: Penguin, 2009), xviii.

2. Kent Dunnington, "The Addict as Modern Prophet," The Gospel Coalition, October 2, 2014, https://www.thegospelcoalition.org/article/addict-as-modern-prophet.

3. Keller, *Counterfeit Gods: The Empty Promises of Money, Sex, and Power, and the Only Hope That Matters*, 23.

Death of a Child

1. Amy Balentine, personal letter, October 30, 2016.

Eating Struggles

1. Penny J. Orr, "Counseling Women with Addictions," in *Women Helping Women: A Biblical Guide to the Major Issues Women Face*, Elyse Fitzpatrick and Carol Cornish, gen. eds. (Eugene, OR: Harvest House, 1997), 401.

2. Emily T. Wierenga, "An Open Letter to My Friends Struggling with Eating Disorders," Desiring God, August 11, 2014, http://www.desiringgod.org/articles/an-open-letter-to-my-friends-struggling-with-eating-disorders.

3. Ibid.

4. Melissa Steffan, "My Perfect Life with Anorexia," *Christianity Today*, August 31, 2012, http://www.christianitytoday.com/women/2012/august/my-perfect-life-with-anorexia.html?paging=off.

Illness

1. Jeremy Linneman, "The Paradox of Chronic Pain," The Gospel Coalition, December 7, 2015, https://www.thegospelcoalition.org/article/the-paradox-of-chronic-pain.

Rape

1. Lindsey A. Holcomb, *Is It My Fault?* (Chicago: Moody, 2014), 83.
2. Jerram Barrs, *Through His Eyes* (Wheaton: Crossway, 2009), 204.

Lust

1. Tripp, *New Morning Mercies*, 196.
2. Kevin DeYoung, *What Does the Bible Really Teach about Homosexuality?* (Wheaton: Crossway, 2015), 127.

Marital Sex

1. Timothy and Kathy Keller, *The Meaning of Marriage*, hardcover ed. (London, UK: Dutton, 2011), 235.
2. Ben Patterson, *Sex and the Supremacy of Christ*, eds. John Piper and Justin Taylor (Wheaton: Crossway, 2005), 17, 55.
3. Nathan Miller, personal letter, October 2016.

Pornography

1. Tim Challies, "7 Lessons from 50 Shades of Grey," blog entry, February 2, 2015, http://www.challies.com/a-la-carte/7-lessons-from-50-shades-of-grey.
2. See the website Fight the New Drug, http://www.fightthenewdrug.com.
3. Halee Gray Scott, "The Porn Paradox," *Christianity Today*, July/August 2016, 38.
4. Ibid., 38.

Sexual Purity

1. Timothy Keller, "The Gospel and Sex."
2. Timothy and Kathy Keller, *The Meaning of Marriage*, paperback ed. (New York: Riverhead, 2011), 256.
3. Ibid., 257.

HEALING WORDS
FROM GOD'S WORD

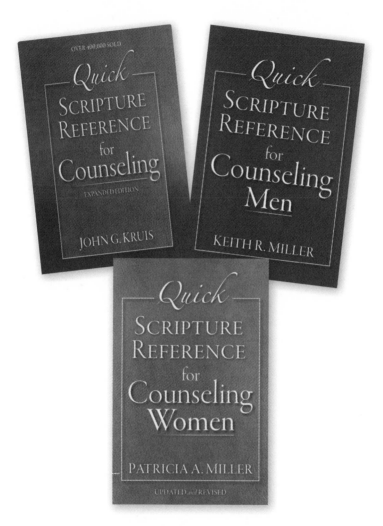

With pertinent Bible passages at the ready, you
will always have just the right words to say—
right when they are most needed.

SCRIPTURE REFERENCE
AT YOUR FINGERTIPS

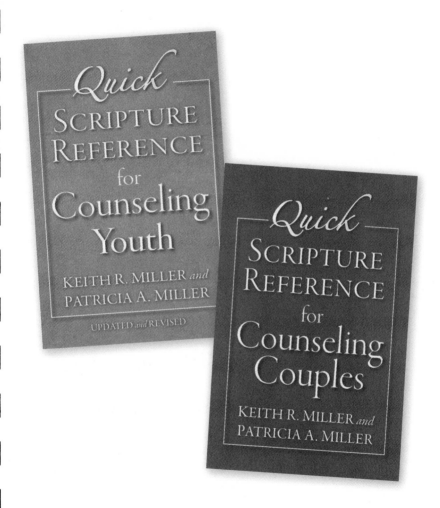

BakerBooks
a division of Baker Publishing Group
www.BakerBooks.com

Available wherever books and ebooks are sold.